WORLD PASS

Expanding English Fluency

Susan Stempleski
Nancy Douglas
James R. Morgan
Kristin L. Johannsen

THOMSON

Australia · Canada · Mexico · Singapore · Spain · United Kingdom · United States

THOMSON

World Pass Advanced, Combo Split A
Susan Stempleski
Nancy Douglas • James R. Morgan • Kristin L. Johannsen

Publisher: Christopher Wenger
Acquisitions Editor: Mary Sutton-Paul
Director of Product Marketing: Amy Mabley
Director of Product Development: Anita Raducanu
Senior Development Editor: Jean Pender
Development Editor: Rebecca Klevberg
Associate Editor: Christine Galvin-Combet
Editorial Assistant: Bridget McLaughlin
Production Editor: Tan Jin Hock

Sr. Print Buyer: Mary Beth Hennebury
International Marketing Manager: Ian Martin
Contributing Development Editor: Barbara Wood
Compositor: Christopher Hanzie, Ronn Lee, TYA Inc.
Photo Researcher: Christopher Hanzie, Ronn Lee
Illustrator: Raketshop Design Studio (Philippines)
Cover/Text Designer: Christopher Hanzie, TYA Inc.
Printer: QuebecorWorld Eusey
Cover Image: TYA Inc. PhotoDisc, Inc.

Printed in Brazil.
1 2 3 4 5 6 7 8 9 10   09 08 07 06 05

For more information contact Thomson Heinle,
25 Thomson Place, Boston, MA 02210 USA, or you
can visit our Internet site at elt.thomson.com

For permission to use material from this text or product,
submit a request online at http://www.thomsonrights.com
Any additional questions about permissions can be submitted
by e-mail to thomsonrights@thomson.com

ISBN: 1-4130-2914-0

Text Credits

Page 21: "'I left home to find home,' interview with Chimamanda Ngozi Adichie," by Carl Wilkinson. Copyright © Guardian Newspapers Limited 2005. Reprinted with permission.; page 71: "On the Tap-Tap," by Kent Annan. Copyright © 2005, Orion Magazine, January/February 2005. Reprinted with permission.

Photo Credits

Unless otherwise stated, all photos are from PhotoDisc, Inc. Digital Imagery © copyright 2006 PhotoDisc, Inc. and TYA Inc. Photos from other sources: page 4: Vincent Kessler/Reuters/Landov; page 5: Morton Beebe/CORBIS; page 6: Laura Cavanaugh/UPI/Landov; page 10: Niviere/EPA/Landov; page 16: (bottom) Royalty-Free/CORBIS; page 20: Nnamdi Chiamogu; page 34: (top) Jacques Langevin/CORBIS SYGMA, (bottom) Jerry Cooke/CORBIS; page 39: (top left) Paul Chinn/San Francisco Chronicle/CORBIS, (top right) Royalty-Free/CORBIS, (bottom) Royalty-Free/CORBIS; page 45: (top left) The Image Bank/Yellow Dog Productions/Getty Images, (top center) Royalty-Free/Andrew Ward/Life File/Photodisc, (top right) Henry Romero/Reuters/Landov, (bottom left) Royalty-Free/Phil Boorman/Photodisc, (bottom center) Reuters/Landov, (bottom right) Ronen Zvulun/Reuters/Landov; page 52: (left) Peter Steiner/CORBIS, (center) Dave G. Houser/CORBIS, (right) Macduff Everton/CORBIS; page 64: (top) Richard Naude/Alamy; page 69: (center) Royalty-Free/Jack Hollingsworth/Photodisc, (right) Dave Turnley/CORBIS; page 72: (top) Reuters/CORBIS, (bottom) Louise Gubb/CORBIS SABA; page 77: (bottom) HIRB

The CNN® logo is a registered trademark of CNN: © & ® 2006. Cable News Network LP, LLLP. A Time Warner Company. All Rights Reserved.

Every effort has been made to trace all sources of illustrations/photos/information in this book, but if any have been inadvertently overlooked, the publisher will be pleased to make the necessary arrangements at the first opportunity.

Acknowledgments

We would firstly like to thank the educators who provided invaluable feedback throughout the development of the *World Pass* series:

Byung-kyoo Ahn, Chonnam National University; Carmen Pulido Alcaraz, Instituto Cultural Mexico-Norteamericano, Guadalajara; Maria Isabel de Souza Lima Baracat, Centro de Comunicação Inglesa, Garça; João Alfredo Bergmann, Instituto Cultural Brasileiro Norte-Americano, Porto Alegre; Elisabeth Blom, Casa Thomas Jefferson; Grazyna Anna Bonomi; Vera Burlamaqui Bradford, Instituto Brasil-Estados Unidos; Flávia Carneiro - Associação Brasil América; Araceli Cabanillas Carrasco, Universidade Autónoma de Sinaloa; Silvania Capua Carvalho, State University of Feira de Santana; Salvador Enriquez Casteñeda, Instituto Cultural Mexico-Norteamericano, Guadalajara; Tânia Branco Cavaignac, Casa Branca Idiomas; Kyung-whan Cha, Chung-Ang University; Chwun-li Chen, Shih Chien University; Ronaldo Couto, SBS, São Paulo; María Teresa Fátima Encinas, Universidad Iberoamericana-Puebla and Universidad Autónoma de Puebla; Maria Amélia Carvalho Fonseca, Centro Cultural Brasil-Estados Unidos, Belém; Sandra Gaviria, Universidad EAFIT; Marina González, Instituto de Lenguas Modernas; Henry W. Grant, Centro Cultural Brasil-Estados Unidos, Campinas; Frank Graziani, Tokai University; Leticia Adelina Ruiz Guerrero, ITESO, Guadalajara; Chi-ying Fione Huang, Ming Chuan University; Shu-fen Huang (Jessie), Chung Hua University; Tsai, Shwu Hui (Ellen), Chung Kuo Institute of Technology and Commerce; Connie R. Johnson, Universidad de las Américas-Puebla; Diana Jones, Instituto Angloamericano; Annette Kaye, Kyoritsu Women's University; Brian Lawrence Kilkenny, PrepaTec, Guadalajara; Lee, Kil-ryoung, Yeungnam University; David Kluge, Kinjo Gakuin University; Lunalva de Fátima Lacerda, Cooplem, Brasília; Nancy H. Lake; Raquel Lambert, CCBEU - Centro Cultural Brasil Estados Unidos de Franca; Hyunoo Lee, Inha University; Amy Peijung Lee, Hsuan Chuang College; Hsiu-Yun Liao, Chinese Culture University; Yuh-Huey Gladys Lin, Chung Hua University; Doraci Perez Mak, União Cultural Brasil-Estados Unidos; Alberto Hernandez Medina, M. Ed., Tecnológico de Monterrey, Guadalajara; Michelle Merritt-Ascencio, University of Guadalajara; Evania A. Netto, ICBEU - São José dos Campos; Eleanor Occeña, Universitaria de Idiomas, Universidad Autónoma del Estado de Hidalgo; Janette Carvalhinho de Oliveira, Universidade Federal do Espírito Santo, Vitória; Laura Pérez Palacio, Tecnológico de Monterrey; Ane Cibele Palma, CCBEU/Interamericano, Curitiba; Mae-Ran Park, Pukyong National University; Joo-Kyung Park, Honam University; Bill Pellowe, Kinki University; Margareth Perucci, Sociedade Brasileira de Cultura Inglesa; Nevitt Reagan, Kansai Gaidai University; Danielle Rêgo, ICBEU - MA; Lesley D. Riley, Kanazawa Institute of Technology; Ramiro Luna Rivera, Tecnológico de Monterrey, Prepa; Marie Adele Ryan, Associação Alumni; Hector Sanchez, PROULEX, Guadalajara; Dixie Santana, Universidad Panamericana, Guadalajara; Rodrigo Santana, CCBEU/Goiânia; Debora Schisler, SEVEN English & Español, São Paulo; Michael Shawback, Ritsumeikan University; Kathryn Singh, ITESM; Sávio Siqueira, ACBEU Salvador; Eric Tejeda, PROULEX, Guadalajara; Grant Trew, Nova Group; Carlos Eduardo Tristão, DISAL; Joaquin Romero Vázquez, Tec de Monterrey, Guadalajara; Liliana Villalobos ME, Universidad Marista de Guadalajara, Universidad de Guadalajara; Michael Wu, Chung Hua University

---

A great many people participated in the making of the *World Pass* series. In particular I would like to thank the authors, Nancy Douglas and James Morgan, for all their hard work, creativity, and good humor. I also extend special thanks to development editor Jean Pender. Thanks are also due to publisher Chris Wenger, acquisitions editor Mary Sutton-Paul, and all the other wonderful people at Thomson ELT who have worked so hard on this project. I am also very grateful to the many reviewers around the world, whose insightful comments on early drafts of the *World Pass* materials were much appreciated.

Susan Stempleski

We'd like to extend a very special thank you to Chris Wenger at Thomson ELT for spearheading the project and providing leadership, support, and guidance throughout the development of the series. And to Jean Pender who edited our materials with speed, precision, and a sense of humor. And also to Susan Stempleski whose extensive experience was reflected in her invaluable feedback that helped to shape the material in this book.

Thanks also go to those on the editorial, production, and support teams who helped to make this book happen: Anita Raducanu, Sally Giangrande, Jin-Hock Tan, Bridget McLaughlin, Christine Galvin-Combet, Rebecca Klevberg, Mary Sutton-Paul, and their colleagues in Asia and Latin America.

I would also like to thank my parents Alexander and Patricia, for their love and encouragement and to my husband Jorge and daughter Jasmine—thank you for your patience and faith in me. I couldn't have done this without you!
Nancy Douglas

I would also like to thank my mother, Frances P. Morgan, for her unflagging support and my father, Lee Morgan Jr., for instilling the love of language and learning in me.
James R. Morgan

I would like to thank my husband, Kevin Millham, for his support and saintly patience.
Kristin L. Johannsen

To the Student

Welcome to *World Pass*! The main goal of this two-level, upper-intermediate/advanced level series is to help you increase your fluency in English. By fluency, I mean the ability to say what you want in more than one way, and to communicate your ideas clearly, confidently, and easily. To help students increase their fluency, *World Pass* focuses on dynamic vocabulary building, essential grammar, and stimulating listening, speaking, and writing activities that emphasize the language people need for real world communication. Features of *World Pass* that emphasize the development of oral and written fluency include the following:

- **Vocabulary Focus sections.** A *Vocabulary Focus* section opens each of the 12 main units and presents topic-related vocabulary along with opportunities to practice using the new words and expressions in a variety of ways. The section includes a "Vocabulary Builder" activity that helps you expand your vocabulary through the use of a particular vocabulary-building tool (e.g., words familes, root words, or compound nouns). Many of the *Vocabulary Focus* sections conclude with an "Ask & Answer" task that can be used as a basis for discussion by pairs, groups, or whole classes of students, and provides opportunities to actively use new vocabulary to express personal ideas, opinions, and experiences.

- **Listening sections.** To become a fluent speaker, you need to be a fluent listener. These sections provide opportunities for you to improve your listening comprehension through active practice with a variety of materials, such as interviews, news reports, and discussions. For added conversational fluency practice, each *Listening* section ends with an "Ask & Answer" discussion task.

- **Language Focus sections.** These sections focus on essential grammar points and provide opportunity for fluency practice through a wide variety of activity types, from more controlled exercises to more personalized, free-response type activities and open-ended communication tasks such as role plays or interviews.

- **Speaking sections.** Each of these sections presents a specific speaking skill or strategy and outlines a communicative activity that helps you to develop your fluency by providing opportunities for you to use new language and vocabulary items in a natural way.

- **Writing sections.** Each of these sections in *World Pass* provide instruction and practice with different kinds of writing such as, business and personal letters, summarizing information, and persuasive writing.

- **Communication sections.** The *Communication* sections that conclude each main unit consolidate and review the language material presented in the unit. Communication tasks vary widely and contribute to the development of fluency by focusing on meaningful speaking practice in activities such as games, presentations, interviews, and discussions.

- **Expansion Pages.** Each unit of *World Pass* is followed by *Expansion Pages*. The *Expansion Pages* are designed for students who want to learn additional vocabulary on their own and to have additional practice with the words and expressions presented in the units. Because the *Expansion Pages* are meant for self-study, they consist of exercises that you can do independently and then check your own answers.

SOME LANGUAGE LEARNING TIPS

Becoming a fluent speaker of English can be challenging, but it can also be a highly rewarding experience. Here are a few tips to help you make the most of the experience.

To increase your vocabulary:
- **Keep a vocabulary log.** Keep a list of new vocabulary items in the back pages of a notebook. From time to time, count up the number of words you have learned. You will be surprised at how quickly the number increases.
- **Use new words in sentences.** To fix news words in your mind, put them into sentences of your own. Do the maximum, not the minimum, with new vocabulary.
- **Make flashcards.** Create vocabulary flashcards that allow you to categorize, label, personalize, and apply new words. Put the words and their definitions on individual cards. Include a sample sentence that shows how the word is used in context.

To improve your speaking skills:
- **Read aloud.** Reading examples and texts out loud is a way of gaining confidence in speaking and letting the patterns of English "sound in your head." Even speaking out loud to yourself can be good practice.
- **Record yourself speaking.** Try recording yourself whenever you can. When you listen to the recording afterwards, don't worry if you sound hesitant or have made mistakes. If you do this several times, you will find that each version is better than the last.

To improve your reading skills:
- **Read passages more than once.** Reading the same reading passage several times will help you increase your reading speed and improve your fluency.
- **Summarize what you read.** When you summarize, you tell the main facts or ideas without giving all the details. Summarizing is a good way to be sure you really understand what you have read.

To improve your writing skills:
- **Increase the amount of writing you do.** For example, you might keep a personal diary in English, write small memos to yourself, or write a summary of a reading passage. The more you write, the more fluent and error-free your writing will become.
- **Analyze different types of writing.** Look at examples of different types of writing you may want to do: essays, formal letters, e-mail messages. Notice the form of the writing and think about what you could imitate to increase your fluency in writing.

To improve your listening comprehension:
- **Listen to recorded material several times.** You aren't expected to understand everything the first time your hear it. If you listen several times, you will probably understand something new each time.
- **Predict what you will hear.** Try to guess what you will hear before you listen. This will help you to focus while you listen and understand more of what you hear.

As you complete each unit of *World Pass*, ask yourself the questions on the **Learning Tips Checklist** below to keep track of the tips you are using and to remind yourself to try using others. To become a truly fluent speaker of English, you will need to practice the different language skills in a variety of ways. Find out what ways work best for you and use them to your advantage.

Susan Stempleski

Sincerely,
Susan Stempleski

Learning Tips Checklist
Which language learning tips did you use as you worked through the unit? Note the ones you used and think about which were most helpful. As you work through the next unit, continue using the helpful ones and try using ones you haven't yet implemented.

Did you . . .
- ❏ record new words in a vocabulary log?
- ❏ try using new words in sentences?
- ❏ make and use vocabulary flashcards?
- ❏ read aloud as often as you could?
- ❏ record and listen to yourself speaking?
- ❏ read reading passages more than once?
- ❏ summarize what you read?
- ❏ write a lot and frequently?
- ❏ analyze and imitate different types of writing?
- ❏ listen to recorded material several times?
- ❏ predict what you would hear before you listened?

Advanced Combo Split A

Scope and Sequence

Lesson A	Vocabulary Focus	Listening	Language Focus	Speaking
Unit 1 Big Screen, Small Screen				
Lesson A 2 Feature films	An online movie club *blockbusters, B-movies, mainstream ...*	A low-budget indie film: Listening for gist and using abbreviations and symbols for taking notes	*Such* and *so*	And the winner is: Managing a discussion
Unit 2 The World Awaits You				
Lesson A 14 On the road *landscape ...*	Dazzling destinations *bustling, atmosphere,* and inferring point of	A photographer's dream: Listening to interviews view; matching speakers with topics	Past modals	Would you mind: Using polite language
Unit 3 School and Beyond				
Lesson A 26 School life	My first year at college *apprehensive, sign up, expectations ...*	School lunches: Listening for details and attitudes	*Hope* and *wish*	That's an interesting question: Practicing interviewing phrases and skills
Review: Units 1–3 38				
Unit 4 Contemporary Issues				
Lesson A 40 In the city	I can get it for free *compensated, unauthorized, unethical ...*	Our cities are growing: Listening for the main point and key words	Past and present unreal conditionals	Without a doubt: Expressing an opinion
Unit 5 In Other Words				
Lesson A 52 Total immersion *master ...*	What languages are you studying? *proficient, immersed,* information	A TV show about language: Listening for topic and specific	Reduced adverb clauses	As you can see: Talking about charts and data
Unit 6 Ordinary People, Extraordinary Lives				
Lesson A 64 Follow your dream!	A well-kept secret *aspirations, sidetracked, channeling ...*	Running ultramarathons: Listening to a personal interview for gist, details, and key words	Reported speech	Today, I'd like to tell you about: Making a presentation to a group using presentation phrases

Review: Units 4–6	76	Grammar Summaries	160	Student Book Answer Key	168
Workbook Activities	2	Skills Index	166	Expansion Pages Answer Key	168
Language Summaries	154				

Lesson B		Get Ready to Read	Reading	Writing	Communication
					Unit 1
Lesson B TV time	7	Reality TV: Discussing popular reality TV shows	A Dose of Reality: Reading an Editorial **Skill**—Inferring an author's opinion or attitude	Writing with topic sentences: Writing a review of a movie or TV program	Is TV controlling your life: Interviewing a partner using a questionnaire Watch this show: Creating a new show and presenting it to a group
Expansion Pages	12				
					Unit 2
Lesson B There and back	19	"Not all those who wander are lost": Analyzing quotes for purpose and meaning	I left home to find home: Reading a personal interview **Skill**—Matching interview questions with answers; guessing meaning from context; pronoun reference	Writing and editing articles: Writing an article and using correction symbols to edit it	Lost at sea: Reading a story, retelling it and predicting the ending The top three: Making a "top three" list for various categories
Expansion Pages	24				
					Unit 3
Lesson B New school, old school	31	School days: Completing a questionnaire about high school education	Education where you live: Reading an online discussion **Skill**—Inferring point of view	Writing an opinion essay: Using a thesis statement and list of advantages and disadvantages to write an opinion essay	One-day workshop: Designing a workshop with a partner Seven wishes and three hopes: Expressing thoughts about the future and past
Expansion Pages	36				
				Review: Units 1–3	38
					Unit 4
Lesson B Conflict resolution	45	What's going on here: Understanding different types of conflicts and potential resolutions	Bullying—what can you do about it: Reading a newspaper article **Skill**—Scanning for specific information; understanding meaning from context; pronoun reference	Expressing an opinion in a short message: Writing a message to post on an online message board	Give and take: Suggesting a compromise
Expansion Pages	50				
					Unit 5
Lesson B Talk to me.	57	It's in the writing: Analyzing writing to detect gender	You just don't get it: Reading an article comparing conversation styles **Skill**—Understanding text organization using contrasts	Report writing: Writing and organizing a report	Debate the issue: Taking part in an organized debate regarding a controversial issue
Expansion Pages	62				
					Unit 6
Lesson B The kindness of strangers	69	A helping hand: Guessing meaning from context	On the Tap-Tap: Reading an online article about a personal experience **Skill**—Guessing meaning from context	Writing a biography: Using general information to write a biography	Person of the Year: Deciding who receives an award and discussing the choices in a group
Expansion Pages	74				

Review: Units 4–6	76	Grammar Summaries	160	Student Book Answer Key	168
Workbook Activities	2	Skills Index	166	Expansion Pages Answer Key	168
Language Summaries	154				

Big Screen, Small Screen

Lesson A | Feature films

1 VOCABULARY FOCUS

An online movie club

 What kinds of movies do you enjoy and what do you find appealing about them?

A Pair work. **Look at the box of informal words used to describe movies. Which ones do you know? With a partner, try to guess what kinds of movies the unfamiliar words refer to.**

chick flick	tearjerker	blockbuster
B-movie	mainstream	indie

B **Some people have joined an online movie club. Read their postings.**

WHAT KINDS OF MOVIES DO YOU LIKE?

Alejandro, Madrid

I'm a sucker for any kind of action movie. I love the big blockbusters with lots of explosions and other things going on. Unfortunately, my girlfriend prefers a good tearjerker—she says it's healthy to cry sometimes. We usually strike a compromise: one week she picks a movie, the next week I get to choose.

Real English
be a sucker for (something) = (informal) have trouble resisting something

I have small children, so I usually see those wholesome films that are "suitable for the entire family." I love my family, but my real interest lies with B-movies. My favorite is Fantastic Creature from Beyond. Most people haven't heard of it, but it's terrific! (I'd tell you about it, but I don't want to give away the ending!)

Carolyn, Vancouver

Real English
chick flick = (slang) movie targeted at a female audience
indie = independent film

Nan, Singapore

Basically, I don't like big-budget mainstream movies. They're so predictable! I prefer the smaller, indie films. Foreign films are great, too, especially when they're shot on some exotic location. There's only one drawback: I don't like to read those subtitles on the screen! Too distracting!

David, Sydney

I enjoy horror or suspense films. On the one hand, I can't stand the tension—it's too nerve-wracking. On the other hand, they're very exciting. Don't tell anyone, but I'd have to say romantic comedies are at the top of my list. I know that they're chick flicks, but they're a kind of guilty pleasure for me.

C Match the expressions on the left with their definitions on the right.

1. blockbuster _d_
2. tearjerker _i_
3. strike a compromise _B_
4. wholesome _J_
5. B-movies _L_
6. give away _F_
7. mainstream _H_
8. shot on location _E_
9. drawback _A_
10. distracting _G_
11. nerve-wracking _C_
12. guilty pleasure _K_

a. disadvantage
b. reach an agreement
c. making you feel tense
d. ~~a very successful book or movie~~
e. not filmed in a studio
f. reveal
g. making it difficult to focus on something
h. popular, appealing to most people
i. a sentimental movie or story that can make people cry
j. considered to have no bad influence
k. something you feel embarrassed about enjoying
l. low-budget films with poor scripts and little-known actors

>> Vocabulary Builder ▲▲

Match the words to form compound nouns that are used when talking about movies. In what kind of movie would you expect to find each of these things?

a. stunts
b. ~~chases~~
c. illness
d. effects
e. romance
f. forces

1. car _b_
2. failed _E_
3. daring _A_
4. superhuman _F_
5. life-threatening _C_
6. special _D_

2 LISTENING

A low-budget indie film

> What's the name of an indie film you've seen? Did you like it? Why or why not?

A Pair work. When you listen and take notes, it's helpful to use abbreviations and symbols. With a partner, look at the ones in the box. What do you think they mean?

> L.A.   P.A.   info   <   >   1ST   w/o   hmtwn   cmdy

B Listen. You will hear an interview with Jesse, a film director. Listen and complete the notes below. Try to use the symbols and abbreviations in A to make your note-taking faster. (CD Tracks 01 & 02)

Jesse	His movie
Age: _23_	Title: _False Information_
Where from: _L.A._	Shot where: _L.A._
1st job in filmmaking: _False Information Production assistant_	Cost: _U/3.200_
	The movie has made: _US 10 mil -0 12 mil._
	Kind of film: _Future Film_

C Listen again. How did Jesse make his film? Circle your answers. There may be more than one answer for some items. (CD Track 03)

1. Money was raised for the film when people read about it / met Jesse / (saw Jesse's short film.)
2. Jesse's cast and crew stayed in (people's homes) / hotels / his hometown hotel.
3. Jesse didn't pay (the actors) / (the cameraman) / to shoot on location.
4. Jesse used celebrities / (friends) / his father in the movie.
5. Jesse based his movie on a book / (his life) / a dream he had.

> ### ► Ask & Answer
> Imagine that you are making a low-budget movie. What would the movie be about? Where would you shoot it? You can't pay the actors. Who would you use in your movie?

D Pair work. Use your notes to retell what you know about Jesse and his movie.

3 LANGUAGE FOCUS

Such and *so*

movie review

👎👎👎👎👍

A Read this exerpt from a movie review. Underline six more examples using *such* or *so*. How does this reviewer feel about the movie?

There was so much hype around this movie before it opened. Unfortunately, it didn't live up to expectations. First of all, the special effects were so distracting that it was hard to focus on the story. And the story was not believable at all. The dialog seemed so forced that this drama sounded more like a comedy. If that wasn't bad enough, then there was the plot; it unfolds in such a confusing series of flashbacks that you can't keep the story straight. I still don't understand it! The worst part, though, is the ending. The movie ends so predictably that you'll wish you had left the theater earlier.

This movie is not a complete disaster, however. The opening scenes are fascinating. The opening is shot in such an interesting way that you'll forget you're watching a movie. And Ella Baker, playing the role of the mother, is phenomenal. She embodies her character with such confidence. Unfortunately, she has so little screen time that we hardly see her.

One recent moviegoer, when asked about this movie, said it for all of us: "I was so disappointed!"

B Look at the phrases you underlined in A. Then write the sentences in which they are used in the chart below.

> **Real English**
> Use *so* and *such* for emphasis.

so + adjective (+ *that* clause)
1. The special effects were so distracting that it was hard to focus on the story.
2. The dialog seemed so forced that this drama sounded more like a comedy
3. The movie ends so predictably that you'll wish you had left the theater earlier

so + adverb (+ *that* clause)
4. I was so disappointed

so + determiner* + noun (+ *that* clause)
5. There was so much hype around this movie before it opened.
6. She has so little screen time that we hardly see her.

such + (*a/an* + adjective) + noun (+ *that* clause)
7. The plot unfolds in such a confusing series of flashbacks that you can't keep the story straight.
8. The opening is shot in such an interesting way that you'll will forget...
9. She embodies her character with such confidence

* determiner = *much/little; many/few*

C Complete these sentences with *so* or *such*.

1. I was __so__ excited to hear that a movie starring Gael García Bernal was opening in my town.
2. I bought __such__ a beautiful outfit for the premiere. You should have seen it!
3. Unfortunately, there were __so__ many people at the premiere that I couldn't get in.
4. I was disappointed that I couldn't see Gael García Bernal at the premiere. He's __such__ a talented actor.
5. Acting is __such__ a difficult profession.
6. First, there's __so__ much competition for acting jobs.
7. Second, there are __so__ few jobs that pay well.
8. Most work pays __so__ poorly that actors have to take a second job to support themselves.

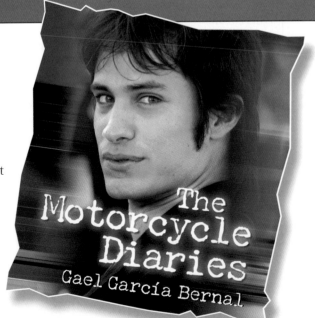

The Motorcycle Diaries
Gael García Bernal

The Castro Theater in San Francisco was built in 1922. It has a gorgeous interior and features live organ music before the movies are shown.

D Read about the Castro Theater in San Francisco.
Then combine the sentences with *so* or *such*.

1. The organ music is popular. People clap and sing along with it. (so)

   The organ music is so popular that people clap and

   sing along with it.

2. It's hard to imagine that the theater is over 80 years old. It's ~~is over 89 year old~~ a well-preserved theater. (such)

   It's hard to imagine that such a well-preserved theater

3. Sometimes the audience will boo loudly at the movie. You can't hear the movie. (so)

   Sometimes the audience will boo so loudly that you can't hear the movie.

4. The atmosphere in the Castro is fun. You should see a movie there. (such)

   The atmosphere in the Castro is such FUNNY that you should see a movie there.

5. The Castro Theater is beautiful. It was designated as a national landmark in 1977. (so)

   the Castro Theater is so beautiful that it was designated as a national landmark

6. Few old movie theaters are left. It's important to preserve old movie theaters. (so) in 1977.

   There are so few old movie theaters that it's important to preserve them.

E Pair work. **Choose one of these two situations and create a role play with your partner.**

Situation 1:
You rented a movie from your local video store. The sound quality of the video was terrible. It was muffled in places and there was a lot of static. Also, you couldn't read some of the subtitles. Return the video and ask for your money back. Explain your reasons.

Situation 2:
You paid for an expensive $25 ticket to see a major blockbuster on an IMAX screen. Inside the theater, there were crowds of noisy kids sitting all around you. It was dirty—the floor was sticky—and there were too many advertisements before the movie even started. Speak to the theater manager and ask for a refund. Explain your reasons.

Grammar X-TRA ▷ *-ed* and *-ing* adjectives

I was **amazed** to hear we won the award.
(I felt amazed.)
The **satisfied** audience left the theater with smiles on their faces.
(The audience felt satisfied.)

That movie is **amazing**.
(That movie causes amazement.)
It was a **satisfying** show.
(The show caused a feeling of satisfaction.)

Pair work. **Tell your partner about a movie you've seen. Include some adjectives. Talk about these topics and others of your own.**

plot   setting   actors   music   special effects

amused
amusing
disappointed
disappointing
entertained
entertaining
excited
exciting
fascinated
fascinating
interested
interesting
shocked
shocking

The plot was very confusing, but I still enjoyed the film because I was fascinated by the special effects.

4 SPEAKING

And the winner is . . .

A Pair work. In your opinion, what makes a movie enjoyable? Memorable? Disappointing? Give examples from movies you've seen. Ask questions about any movies your partner mentions that you haven't seen.

B Pair work. Look at this list of international film awards that are given out each year and answer the questions below with a partner. Check your answers on page 168.

INTERNATIONAL FILM AWARDS
The Academy Awards
The Cannes Film Festival
The BAFTA Film Awards
Hong Kong Film Awards

1. What is the name of the small statue that is given to winners at the Academy Awards? _Oscar_

2. What country hosts the Cannes Film Festival? _France_

3. What does BAFTA stand for? (complete) _British_ Academy of Film and _Television_ Arts

4. In what year was the first Hong Kong Film Awards held: 2001, 1991, or 1982? _1982_

C Group work. Imagine that you represent *The International Movie Fans' Association*. Follow the steps below.

1. You are in charge of giving away the "Decade Awards." You must choose the five best movies of the last ten years.

2. Work together to choose the winner for each category. Use language from the box below to manage the discussion.

3. Agree on your choice for each category.

Most romantic movie: _____

Most exciting movie: _____

Most frightening movie: _____

Funniest movie: _____

Your own category: _____

Managing a discussion		
Requesting clarification:	**Taking your turn:**	**Keeping the discussion moving:**
Sorry, I'm not sure I understand.	*Can I just add something here?*	*To get back to our topic . . .*
Why do you say that?	*I have a point I'd like to make.*	*Let's hear what someone else*
Can you clarify your reason?	*Sorry to interrupt, but . . .*	*has to say.*
		We only have five minutes left.

D Class activity. Take turns explaining your group's awards to the class. Did any groups make the same decisions? Were there any surprising awards?

Big Screen, Small Screen

Lesson B	TV time

1 GET READY TO READ

Reality TV

What are two of the most popular reality shows right now? Why do you think these shows are popular? With a partner, make a list of reasons.

A Pair work. **Read about the four reality shows below. Can you spot the reality show that's fake (not an actual reality show)? Explain your ideas to a partner. Then check your answer on page 168.**

TV Guide

Doctors' Diaries is a docu-drama that examines the events that take place in a busy hospital as well as the stories of the doctors, nurses, and medics who work there.

In each episode of **Blind Love**, a person sets up his or her pet on a blind date with another person's pet. The show follows the romantic, sometimes disastrous, outcome.

The Call tells the stories of three actors competing for roles in actual TV and film productions. Who will get that first big break?

The World's Most Daring Robberies presents the boldest bank robbers ever caught on tape and their infamous crime sprees. The program includes interviews with the FBI, bank tellers, and even the robbers themselves.

B Pair work. **What do each of these adjectives mean? Discuss your ideas with a partner. Use your dictionary to help you.**

addictive	disturbing	heartfelt
compelling	dramatic	inspiring
cutthroat	entertaining	shocking

C Pair work. **Discuss these questions with a partner.**

1. Which of the words in B would you use to describe the shows in A?
2. In your opinion, which of the reality shows in A would be most popular? Why?
3. Which one(s) would you watch? Which wouldn't you watch? Why?

I think the most entertaining show would be . . .

World Link

On average, camera crews for reality TV shows shoot 100 hours of video for every hour of the show! Without good editing, viewers would lose interest long before they found out who the winner was!

Source: *Bunim-Murray Productions*

A Dose of Reality

A   Read the two summaries below. Then read the article on page 9 and check (✓) the summary that best describes the article.

❑   Early critics believed that interest in reality shows wouldn't last long. Today, though, these shows are more popular than ever and can be seen all over the world. Nevertheless, people are beginning to question whether or not this kind of "reality entertainment" is suitable—especially for younger viewers.

☑   Reality shows are often advertised as a genuine look at the lives of real people. The fact is, though, that many of these shows are not as "real" as they claim to be. A variety of techniques are used—including using scripted dialog and editing scenes—to make the shows more dramatic and interesting to the public.

B   Read the article again. Then complete each sentence by circling the correct answer.

1.   The problem with filming real people for a reality show is that it can be very expensive / most people's lives aren't that interesting / it takes a long time to do.
2.   Some reality show producers have hired professional actors / filmmakers / scriptwriters to help those being filmed say things in a more dramatic way.
3.   Gideon Horowitz, who injured himself while filming *The Restaurant*, was asked to resign from the show / refilm the fall that broke his elbow / return to work 24 hours later.
4.   On reality shows, footage is often edited to make people on the show look more attractive / seem to have a certain kind of personality / appear to be less nervous on screen.
5.   A woman on *The Apprentice*, was loved / disliked by the public because she was always / never seen smiling and laughing on the show.

C   Find these words in the reading. Then write each in the correct place in the chart below.

authentic (line 33)   staged (line 63)   contrived (line 82)
unrehearsed (line 36)   scripted (line 66)

Describes something that is real or genuine	Describes something that is fake or invented
authentic unrehearsed	staged scripted contrived

D   Pair work. Check (✓) the statements below that you think the author of the reading would probably say. What information in the reading helped you make your choices? Discuss your ideas with a partner.

1.   Reality show producers will do just about anything to boost ratings. ☑
2.   One good thing about these shows is that you do see people expressing genuine, heartfelt emotion. ❑
3.   I used to dislike reality shows, and frankly, I still do. ❑
4.   I think that reality shows ought to be banned from television. ❑

Inferring an author's opinion or attitude

The author may not always state his or her opinion directly. Often a reader must infer, or make guesses about it, using the information that is available in the text.

▶ Ask & Answer

Was any of the information in the reading surprising to you? Why or why not? If you could be on a reality show, which kind would you appear on? Why? Which kind would you avoid?

Real English

contestant = person on a
game show who competes
against others to win
something

Real English

average Joe = typical man
nerdy = socially awkward

A Dose of Reality

Colin Flemming

I was on the bus the other morning on my way to work when I was distracted by two young women chatting behind me.

"... I know, did you see the clothes he had on?" the first one laughed.

5 Must be talking about some poor guy at school, I thought.

"And when he started singing ... I almost died I laughed so hard!" Now I was feeling really bad for the guy.

"The thing is," says girl number two, now somewhat seriously, "if *this* guy can get on TV—especially *American Idol*, anyone can. I think 10 he's totally inspiring in a way."

"Yeah, you're right," agreed number one. "He couldn't sing, but there was something very real ... you know, genuine and sweet, about him ..."

Oh, now I get it. They're not laughing at someone they actually 15 know ... they're talking about some guy who was on the reality show *American Idol*. I should've known. Based on the British show *Pop Idol*, *American Idol* is one of the top-rated programs in the U.S. For those of you who've been living in a cave for the last several years and have never heard of the show, it's basically a talent contest in which the 20 winner is given a recording deal. This career-launching reality show has become so popular that it has produced various spin-offs (e.g., *Canadian Idol* and *Australian Idol*) as well as shows with similar formats including *Fama* in Brazil, *Operación Triunfo* in Argentina and Spain, *La Academia* in Mexico, and *Factory of Stars* in Russia.

25 Early critics of reality TV (OK ... I was one of them) believed that the popularity of shows like *Idol, Survivor, Big Brother*, and others would be short-lived. Guess what? We were wrong. Once popular primarily in the U.K. and the U.S., one can now tune in to a variety of reality shows all over the world. There are courtroom dramas and 30 makeover specials, historical re-creations, and kitchen competitions. You name it ... and there's probably a reality show about it.

So, what makes shows like these so popular? For many, it's the idea that what they're watching is somehow authentic. Sure, there's a bit of fantasy thrown in, but unlike a sit-com or TV 35 drama, viewers believe that what they're seeing are regular people in unscripted, unrehearsed situations: young go-getters vying for a job, couples meeting and falling in love, singers competing to win a recording contract, or castaways on an island struggling to survive. Episodes are full of dramatic moments, surprising twists, heartbreaking 40 losses, and thrilling wins. And it's all real. Or is it?

The ironic truth about a lot of reality TV is that it relies more on fiction than fact to get the public to watch. Reality show producers are interested in filming the average Joe going on a date or winning that million—as long as the footage can be used to boost ratings. The 45 unfortunate reality, though, is that Joe's life doesn't always provide the compelling highs and lows that make a TV show interesting to the public.

And so, what can a reality show producer do? Some have gone as far as to bring professional scriptwriters on to the set to help 50 those being filmed to "express themselves better." While subjects aren't necessarily being encouraged to act, they are being "helped" to see that instead of saying, for example, "That was scary.", it might be more interesting to say "I was so *afraid* that my heart almost stopped!" The feelings are still the same, say the shows' producers. It's just that 55 they're a little more *heartfelt* now.

Reality show producers will also use "creative editing" to ensure that there's plenty of drama (great for ratings) in every episode. The program *The Restaurant*, for example, focused on celebrity chef Rocco DiSpirito and his high-profile establishment in New York City. 60 During filming, employee Gideon Horowitz fell and broke his elbow. Perfect, right? Not quite. When Horowitz returned to work, the show's producers, who felt that his fall hadn't been dramatic enough, asked him to refilm it. The staged fall was included in the show that aired for the public.

65 Creative editing is also used to make those being filmed more like characters in a scripted TV show ("the good girl," "the nerdy guy," "the party animal"). And the public loves it. On the first season of *The Apprentice*—a show in which billionaire businessman Donald Trump interviewed different job applicants to head one of his companies— 70 the show's producers edited large amounts of footage to make one of the job applicants appear to be a nasty, scheming woman. According to Ms. Omarosa Manigault-Stallworth, all instances of her smiling or talking in a friendly way with other contestants were edited out of the final footage shown on TV. For a time, Stallworth was hailed as "the 75 most hated woman on television"—an image that she claims was created by the show's producers and editors. In the end, Stallworth didn't get the job, but *The Apprentice* was a huge hit—thanks in great part to Stallworth's "character" on the show.

What does this all mean? Am I saying that reality TV is bad or 80 that you shouldn't watch it? Not at all. Just keep in mind the next time you tune in that many of the scenes that make you laugh, cry, cheer, or shout, were probably contrived by the show's producers to get that exact reaction. Just like on your favorite scripted TV show.

3 WRITING

Writing with topic sentences

A Read the DVD review from a web site. Fill in the best topic sentence for each paragraph.

Paragraph 1
- *The Last Samurai* features actors from Japan and the U.S.
- *The Last Samurai* is a good movie, but not a great one.
- *The Last Samurai* is one of the best movies I've ever seen.

Paragraph 2
- The movie's plot is loosely based on Japanese history.
- This is definitely one of Tom Cruise's best movies.
- The samurai were warriors in traditional Japan.

Paragraph 3
- This was one of the most popular movies of the year.
- *The Last Samurai* has wonderful scenery and costumes.
- There's a lot to enjoy in *The Last Samurai*.

---

myDVDstore.com

The Last Samurai

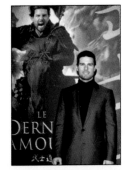

PhilB says: ★ ★ ★ ★

The Last Samurai is a good movie, but not a great one.

It's a drama that mixes entertainment with a message about honor and loyalty. As entertainment, it's terrific, but the message doesn't really come through.

The movie's plot is loosely based on Japanese history.

The Last Samurai is about an American soldier named Nathan Algren (Tom Cruise) who goes to Japan in 1876 to help the Emperor's army catch a samurai warlord named Katsumoto (played by Ken Watanabe), who is challenging the government's authority. Algren is captured by Katsumoto, and comes to understand the samurai way of life that Katsumoto is fighting to preserve. I won't give away the ending, but I thought the final battle scene was totally unrealistic.

There's a lot to enjoy in THE LAST SAMURAI.

It's filled with great camera work, nice action scenes, and plenty of drama. The acting (particularly Watanabe's) is superlative. The big problem is the simplistic story. Why would a samurai army need help from an American? Overall, I gave this 2003 movie four out of five stars. This is a fun DVD for a Saturday night when there's nothing good on TV—just don't think too hard about what it all means.

Write your own review! Click here

B Write a review for myDVDstore.com of a movie or TV program that you especially liked—or disliked. Give it a star rating of one to five stars. Include a topic sentence for each paragraph.

Paragraph 1: Introduce the movie or program.
Paragraph 2: Describe the movie or program.
Paragraph 3: Explain the reasons for your rating and say who might enjoy this DVD.

C Pair work. Exchange reviews with a partner. Did your partner's review make you want to buy, or not buy, this DVD? Why? Make suggestions for improving or clarifying the review.

4 COMMUNICATION

Activity 1: Is TV controlling your life?

A Pair work. **Interview a partner using the questionnaire below. Ask your partner to explain his or her answers.**

How often do you . . .	often	sometimes	never
1. watch television while doing other things (e.g., eating, doing homework, talking on the phone)?			
2. come home and immediately turn on the television?			
3. schedule your day or week around shows you want to watch on TV?			
4. hum or sing along to commercials that are on TV?			
5. talk to friends about certain TV shows and the people on them?			
6. record TV shows so that you can watch them later?			
7. fall asleep with the TV on?			

B Pair work. **Calculate your partner's score. Then read the description below to your partner.**

> often = 3 points   sometimes = 2 points   never = 1 point

19–21 points	Wow . . . you watch so much TV that it's hard to believe you don't have it on now. My friend, TV is controlling your life. Time to break free and find a new hobby!
11–18 points	Congratulations! Though some of you may watch more TV than you probably should—especially if you scored 16 to 18 points—your life is definitely not ruled by what's on and when.
7–10 points	No doubt about it . . . you're the one in control, not the television. The only drawback may be that you won't be able to chat with your friends about TV shows.

Activity 2: Watch this show!

A Pair work. **You and your partner are going to create a new reality TV show. Discuss the questions below. Assume that the show will be on once a week for an hour.**

1. What kind of reality show is it going to be (e.g., talent contest, docu-drama, makeover special, dating competition, historical re-creation)?
2. Who is the show's target audience (children, teenagers, young adults, adults)?
3. What exactly will happen on the show?
4. Why do you think people will watch your new show? Use three adjectives (e.g., compelling, heartfelt, shocking) to describe the show and explain your answer.

B Group work. **Using the information in A, create a two-minute sales pitch for your show and present it to the class. Your classmates will listen, take notes, and ask you questions.**

C Pair work. **After everyone has presented their shows, look over your notes and discuss the questions below with a partner.**

1. In your opinion, which of your classmates' reality shows would most likely be picked up by a TV network? Why?
2. Which one(s) would you watch?

 **Check out the CNN® video.** **Practice your English online at** elt.thomson.com/worldpass

Unit 1: Big Screen, Small Screen

A Complete the sentences with movie terms from the box. Use your dictionary as necessary.

> dubbed   subtitled   on location   soundtrack   credits
> studios   screenplays   flashback   stunts

1. At the end of the movie, you can read the names of the actors and of all the people who worked on the film in the __credits__ .
2. When a movie is __Dubbed__ , actors speak the dialog in a language different from the original.
3. For many popular movies, you can buy a CD of the music from the __Soundtrack__ .
4. In a __Subtitled__ movie, you read the dialog translated into another language at the bottom of the screen.
5. It's sometimes very expensive to shoot a movie __on location__ in the actual place where the story takes place.
6. During a __Flashback__ in a movie, the action goes back to an earlier time in the story.
7. Special actors do dangerous __stunts__ such as crashing cars or jumping out of burning buildings.
8. Many movies are made in __studios__ , which have areas that look like different parts of the world.
9. The __Screenplas__ for some famous movies are based on popular novels.

B Match the questions and answers about movies.

1. What kind of movie is it? _G_
2. What's it about? _h_
3. When was it made? _c_
4. Where is it from? _F_
5. Who's in it? _B_
6. Who's it by? _A_
7. Where is it showing? _E_
8. How is it? _D_

a. A new director that I've never heard of.
b. Tom Cruise and Julia Roberts.
c. A few years ago, I think.
d. Kind of slow at first, but the end is really scary!
e. At CineClub, downtown.
f. China. It's subtitled in English.
g. A detective story.
h. Two guys who are in love with the same woman.

> **I didn't know that!**
> *Humor* comes from the Latin word for "liquid." Centuries ago, philosophers believed that people's personalities were controlled by the liquids in their bodies. If these liquids were out of balance, the personality would be unbalanced too. Originally, a *humorous* person was strange or odd. Over time, the meaning changed to someone who could make other people laugh.

C Here are some more common abbreviations and symbols that can be used in taking notes while listening. Determine the meaning of each and write it on the line.

1. w/ __with__
2. 2nd __second__
3. sm _____
4. lg _____
5. abt __about__
6. # __number__
7. btw __between__
8. + __plus__

D Review the words from the reading "A Dose of Reality" on page 9. Then write them next to their meanings.

distracted (line 2)	spin-off (line 21)	episode (line 39)	producer (line 48)
genuine (line 12)	vying (line 36)	footage (line 44)	nasty (line 71)

1. real, not artificial or false ___Genuine___
2. a TV series based on another earlier series ___spin-off___
3. one part in a continuing TV story ___episode___
4. have your attention taken away by something ___distracted___
5. competing with someone to get something ___vying___
6. the person who finances and plans a TV program ___producer___
7. film of a particular scene or event ___footage___
8. unkind and unpleasant ___nasty___

E Complete the paragraph with the correct forms of the TV words in the box.

antenna	remote	show	host
cable	satellite	network	channel

    My boyfriend says I'm a complete couch potato, and the fact is, I'm fascinated by TV. I can sit for hours with the **(1)** ___remote control___ in my hand, just switching from one program to another. In my country, there are only two TV **(2)** ___channels network___, and they're really boring. One of them, TVN, is run by the government, and the other is independent. Last year my parents finally got **(3)** ___cable antenna___ TV, so now we can watch 40 different **(4)** ___channels___. I would really like to get **(5)** ___cable___ TV, but we would need a special **(6)** ___satellite___ outside and that's a problem. We live in an apartment and there's no good place to put it outside. There's one **(7)** ___show___ that I just have to see every day. It's called *Everybody's Talking* and there are always a lot of interesting guests. The show's **(8)** ___host___ is a comedian named Johnny Sung, and he's SO funny!

In Other Words

The audience (a collective noun) is the group of people at a theater: *The audience applauded at the end of the movie.*
Spectators watch a sports event: *All of the spectators were wearing blue and white, their team's colors.*
Viewers are people who watch a TV program: *An announcement before the program warned viewers that it contained scenes that were not appropriate for children.*

A review is a written evaluation of a movie, TV program, book, etc.: *The new movie with Tom Hanks got great reviews in all the newspapers.*
A critic is a person who writes reviews: *My sister is a movie critic for* Today *magazine.*
A critique is a detailed written explanation of problems and their causes: *Dr. Lee is writing a critique of the health care system in our country.*

Watch out!

see and watch
You can *watch* TV, or you can *see* something on TV, but you don't "see TV."
    We watched TV until midnight last night.
    I saw an interview with the president on TV.
    I saw television after dinner.

1 VOCABULARY FOCUS
Dazzling destinations

 Take one minute and write down the places in the world you would most like to visit. Compare your list with a partner. Discuss the places you chose.

A Pair work. **Read this blurb about a new travel book. Discuss with a partner. Would you buy the book? Why or why not?**

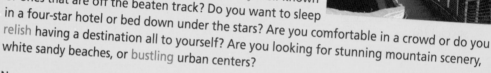

Are you restless—you can't sit still and don't know why?
Maybe it's time to take a trip!

Do you prefer visiting places that are relatively well-known or ones that are off the beaten track? Do you want to sleep in a four-star hotel or bed down under the stars? Are you comfortable in a crowd or do you relish having a destination all to yourself? Are you looking for stunning mountain scenery, white sandy beaches, or bustling urban centers?

No matter what your tastes may be, we've got it covered in this latest edition of *Dazzling Destinations*. We've surveyed the world's best travel writers and come up with these twenty must-see places and activities for your reading pleasure. And, with over two hundred glossy photographs that are guaranteed to grab your attention, you won't be able to put this book down!

Our award-winning staff of writers and photographers have had firsthand experiences visiting all of these destinations. The information is up-to-date and tells you which sites to take in and which ones to avoid.

In this book, you'll find many places which have become household names, such as the Great Wall of China or Carnaval in Rio. We also feature less familiar destinations, such as the Pushkar Camel Fair in India. And it's not all serious travel tips: you'll also learn all about the Coney Island hot dog eating contest! This book is a traveler's dream—the next best thing to actually being there.

"The photos in this book are so good that you can soak up the atmosphere of each place without leaving your own armchair!"
Sylvia Feinstein, *World Traveler News*

"There are a lot of wonderful sites in the world and these photos show the beauty of the landscape so perfectly. This book is hypnotic—I couldn't put it down!"
M. Perretti, *travelxyz.com*

ISBN 0-X384-XXXX-X

9 XXXX384 425XXX6

New Edition   Made in U.S.A.

B Pair work. **Ask and answer these questions with a partner. Use a dictionary for words you don't know.**

1. Are you a restless person or are you easily satisfied?
2. How would you answer the questions in the first paragraph of the blurb on page 14?
3. In your opinion, what travel destination would be guaranteed to be fun?
4. Have you had firsthand experience traveling somewhere exciting? What things did you take in when you were there?
5. What travel destinations are household names in your country?
6. What two or three words would you use to describe the atmosphere of your city?
7. What kind of photos do you prefer in a travel book: local handicrafts, people, or landscapes?
8. The book in A is described as *hypnotic*. What do you think that word means?

Real English
up for (something) = willing or capable of doing something

C Pair work. **These people are looking for their own "dazzling destinations."**
What destination would you suggest for each person? Compare your ideas with a partner.

Vera

"It should be physically challenging or even dangerous. I'm a real thrill-seeker."

Sean

"I'm not single anymore, so it should be a place that's appropriate for the entire family . . . but interesting for us adults too."

Monique

"I'm up for going anywhere that has a lot of eating or dancing—the two things I love to do most!"

 Vocabulary Builder

These words all end in *-less*. Write them in the chart. Then complete the sentences. Not all words are used.

~~ageless~~   ~~countless~~   ~~meaningless~~   ~~priceless~~
~~childless~~   effortless   ~~powerless~~   timeless

-less = lacking something	*-less* = exceeding a category
childless Powerless Effortless	ageless countless, Timeless meaningless PRiceless

1. We're _PowerLess_ to do anything about the situation. We should give up.
2. She may be almost 60 years old, but there's a kind of _AGELESS_ beauty about her.
3. The time I spent with my grandmother before she died was _TIMELESS_.
4. The government is worried about the increasing number of _childless_ couples.
5. He's such an accomplished mountain climber. He makes it look _EffoRTLess_.

2 LISTENING
A photographer's dream

Have you ever taken a memorable travel photo?
What was special about it? Describe it to your partner.

A Pair work. **Each of these three photographs appeared in the book** *Dazzling Destinations*. **Where do you think each photo was taken? Discuss with a partner.**

B **You will hear three photographers talking about their work. Listen and match each photographer to the photo that he or she took. Write the number in the box.** (CD Tracks 04 & 05)

1. Leslie   2. Olga   3. Diego

C **Listen again. Circle the statements that each person would say. There may be more than one answer.** (CD Track 06)

1. Leslie
   a. I'm patient.
   b. I visit each place once.
   c. I like contrast in colors.

2. Olga
   a. It took me a long time to figure out the kind of photos I wanted to take.
   b. I'm not into the latest photography techniques.
   c. The development process is easy.

3. Diego
   a. I photograph birds mainly.
   b. I think people and animals have a lot in common.
   c. There was a lot to see in Antarctica.

> **Ask & Answer**
> What places do you think are a photographer's dream? Why?

3 LANGUAGE FOCUS
Past modals

A Pair work. **Hilary is meeting Sam at the airport. Read their conversation and notice the phrases in blue. Then, with a partner, circle the correct answers in the sentences on page 17.**

Hilary: Hi, Sam. Have you been waiting long?
Sam: About an hour and a half. My flight got in early.
Hilary: Oh no. You should've phoned me! I would've come to the airport earlier.
Sam: I tried calling you at home, but there wasn't any answer.
Hilary: I must've left already. You could've tried my cell phone.
Sam: That's true, but I left your number at home. I should've written it down!
Hilary: Yeah, it would've been easier. I was waiting at the wrong place and when I didn't see you, I thought "he couldn't have arrived yet. His plane isn't due until 2:00." Anyway, how are you?
Sam: Good. Listen, I could've booked a hotel before I arrived, but I thought I'd wait and ask for your advice. Can you recommend a place to stay?
Hilary: Don't be silly, Sam! You're staying with us. Now, do you need help with your luggage?

1. When Hilary says "You should've phoned me," she is giving Sam a **strong / polite** suggestion.
2. When Hilary says "I would've come to the airport earlier," she is showing her **willingness / unwillingness** to do something.
3. When Hilary says "I must've left already," she is giving **advice / a conclusion**.
4. When Hilary says "You could've tried my cell phone," she is giving a **strong / polite** suggestion.
5. When Sam says "I should've written it down," he is **giving advice / expressing regret**.
6. When Hilary says "He couldn't have arrived yet," she is expressing **possibility / impossibility (or disbelief)**.
7. When Sam says "I could've booked a hotel," he is expressing **possibility / impossibility**.

B Read this story about Blaine's first trip to New York fifteen years ago. On a separate piece of paper, answer the questions below using the modal phrases from **A**.

> My first day in New York was a disaster. I took a taxi from the airport into the city and it was very expensive. I didn't have a hotel reservation, so I went to the youth hostel looking for a room. They were booked up. It took me three hours and many phone calls before I could find a place to stay. I was hungry, so that evening I put my wallet in my back pocket and went out to dinner. I got lost because I didn't have a subway map and I was by myself. When I finally got to the restaurant, I was famished and I ordered a lot of food. When I went to pay, I realized my wallet was missing! I couldn't believe it!

1. What could Blaine have done when he got lost?
2. What do you think happened to his wallet?
3. How do you think he felt when he realized his wallet was missing?
4. Is there any advice you would have given Blaine at the time?
5. What would you have done differently if you had taken the trip to New York?

C Pair work. **Which sentence logically follows the first one? Circle your answer. Then explain your answers to a partner.**

1. She shouldn't have called him.
   a. I know. What a mistake!
   b. Maybe she can do it tomorrow.

2. Jim couldn't have gone to Hawaii last week.
   a. He was in the office every day.
   b. He might have been in the office.

3. How was the concert last night?
   a. It was great. I could go, but I didn't.
   b. I don't know. I could have gone, but I didn't.

4. Where's Tom?
   a. His computer is turned off. He must have left already.
   b. His computer is turned off. He must not have left already.

5. What would you have done in that situation?
   a. I don't know, but I would've done what you did.
   b. I don't know, but I wouldn't have done what you did.

D Read the sentences. Circle the letter that shows the one incorrect part of each sentence and correct it.

1. You shouldn't have leave the car headlights on. Now the battery is dead.
       A   B   C   D
2. If I were you, I would've tell him the truth about your travel plans.
       A   B   C   D
3. I could've went to a bustling city, but then I wouldn't have met any of the local people.
       A   B   C   D
4. I think the projector must not have been work well because they never showed the in-flight movie.
                              A   B   C   D
5. I'm not sure, but he could board the flight in Miami. We'll have to check with the airline.
           A   B   C   D

E Read this letter to the editor of a travel magazine. What advice would you give to "Jet Lagged in Jakarta"?

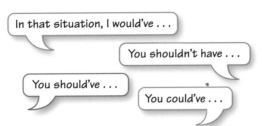

In that situation, I would've . . .

You shouldn't have . . .

You should've . . .

You could've . . .

> Dear Editor,
> I recently took a trip to Jakarta. I booked the cheapest flight I could find. It was an overnight flight and they didn't serve any meals. I was so hungry! By the time we landed, I had a terrible headache. I got to my hotel by 2:00 P.M. and took a two-hour nap. That night, I couldn't sleep at all. I didn't enjoy my trip because I had terrible jet-lag. Can you give me some advice?
> — "Jet Lagged in Jakarta"

Grammar X-TRA ▶ Showing regret in the past with *wish*

- I *wish* I **hadn't** lost my passport. It was such a hassle to get a new one.
- We didn't arrive on time. I *wish* we **had**.

Pair work. Tell your partner about a time you took a trip and something went wrong. Your partner will suggest things that you could've or should've done differently.

A: I flooded the bathtub in our hotel room last summer.
B: Really? You should've watched the water more closely.
A: Yeah, I wish I'd done that.

---

4 SPEAKING

Would you mind . . .

A Group work. Read this phone conversation. Look at the underlined expressions where the speakers are using overly casual or inappropriate language. Discuss what they could say to sound more polite.

Operator:	Thank you for calling the Sun Coast Hotel. (1) Who do you want to talk to?
Jennie:	(2) Reservations.
Operator:	(3) OK. (4) Hold on a minute.
Clerk:	Good afternoon, (5) I'm Cassandra. (6) What do you want?
Jennie:	Hello? (7) How much is a double room?
Clerk:	The rate is $125 for a standard double.
Jennie:	Oh . . . (8) That's too expensive.
Clerk:	Well, we also offer a special weekend rate of $70 for Saturday and Sunday nights.
Jennie:	That sounds perfect. Do you have a double room available for March 16th and 17th?

Clerk:	Just a moment . . . yes, we do.
Jennie:	Also, (9) is your hotel on the beach?
Clerk:	Yes, it is. We have our own private beach for guests.
Jennie:	Perfect! Then I'd like to make a reservation.
Clerk:	May I have your name, please?
Jennie:	Jennie Tranh.
Clerk:	(10) How do you spell that?
Jennie:	That's T-R-A-N-H.
Clerk:	And could I have your credit card number, please?
Jennie:	Sure—it's . . .

B Group work. Now look at the polite language in the box. Match each expression to its underlined counterpart in A. Then practice the polite version of the conversation.

a. I'm afraid that's a little out of my price range. ___
b. How may I direct your call? ___
c. How may I help you? ___
d. Certainly. ___
e. I was wondering whether your hotel is located on the beach or not. ___
f. This is Cassandra. ___
g. Would you mind spelling that for me? ___
h. One moment, please. ___
i. Could you please tell me the cost of a double room? ___
j. I'd like to speak with someone in Reservations, please. ___

C Pair work. Choose one of the hotels in the photos. With a partner, work together to role-play a phone conversation to make a reservation.

Mountain View Lodge

Skytop Hotel

River Guest House

The World Awaits You

Lesson B | There and back

1 GET READY TO READ

"Not all those who wander are lost."

WARM UP

What are some reasons why people travel?
Think of a trip you have taken. Why did you go?

A Pair work. Read these quotes and then discuss the
questions below with a partner.

> Not all those who wander are lost.
> ~J. R. R. Tolkien

> A man travels the world over in search of
> what he needs, and returns home to find it.
> ~ George Moore

> Not I - not anyone else, can travel that road
> for you. You must travel it for yourself.
> ~ Walt Whitman

World Link

> Residents of popular tourist destinations must
> sometimes feel as if visitors are crawling around
> everywhere. It's no wonder the Anangu Aboriginal
> people of Australia sometimes call tourists
> "minga," a word which also means "ants."
>
> Source: *traveloasis.com*

> Wherever you go, the sky is the same color.
> ~Persian saying

> The real voyage of discovery
> consists not in seeking new
> landscapes, but in having new eyes.
> ~Marcel Proust

1. What do you think each quote means?
2. Which quote do you like or agree with most? Why? Are there any quotes that you disagree with? Why?
3. Can you think of any other sayings related to travel and journeys?

B Pair work. You're going to read an interview with a woman from Nigeria. How much do you know about this country?
Take the quiz below and then compare ideas with a partner. Check your answers on page 168.

The Nigeria Quiz

1. Nigeria has the largest / smallest population of any African country.
2. The official language of Nigeria is Yoruba / English / French.
3. Skiing / Cricket / Soccer is the country's most popular sport.
4. Nigeria's largest export is clothing / oil / exotic fruit.
5. Many Nigerian dishes tend to be hot and spicy / plain and watery.
6. Which of the following people was born in Nigeria?
   the musician Sade / actress Halle Berry / Secretary-General of the United Nations, Kofi Annan

I left home to find home

A Pair work. You are going to read an interview with author Chimamanda Ngozi Adichie. First look at her photo and read the information about her. Then read the title of the interview on page 21. Discuss with your partner what you think the reading is going to be about.

Chimamanda Ngozi Adichie was born in Nigeria in 1977. Her short stories and novels have won or been nominated for several important literary awards including the Booker Prize and the Orange Prize for fiction.

B Pair work. Now read the interview and write the questions below on the correct lines in the text. Then compare your answers with a partner.

Will you travel more now?
Do you remain rooted in Nigeria or are you keen to travel?
Has travel given you a strong sense of being Nigerian?
When did you make your first trip outside Nigeria?
What do you love about Nigeria?
Have you traveled within Africa?

C Read the interview again. Then using your own words, answer the questions below on a separate piece of paper.

1. How old was Ms. Adichie the first time she traveled abroad? Where did she go and how long did she stay there?
2. Why was she a little disappointed by her first trip abroad?
3. How old was Ms. Adichie when she moved to the U.S. to live? How long did she live there and how did she feel about it?
4. How did living in the U.S. change Ms. Adichie? What did she learn by living there?
5. What are the things that Ms. Adichie loves most about her country?
6. Where did Ms. Adichie go in 2002? Did she enjoy the trip? Why or why not?
7. Where would Ms. Adichie like to go next?

D Find the words or phrases in the reading. Then circle the word or phrase each is most similar to.

1. *wanderlust* (line 7)	feeling of boredom	desire to travel
2. *can-do* (line 13)	doubt and concern	optimism and strength
3. *rooted* (line 18)	settled, connected to a place	unattached, free
4. *surreal* (line 27)	familiar	weird, bizarre
5. *sorted out* (line 31)	understood, solved	hid or concealed

E Fill in the blanks below with the correct word or phrase from the reading.

1. In line 11, *there* refers to _____.
2. In line 16, *they* refers to _____.
3. In line 21, *It* refers to _____.
4. In line 23, *there* refers to _____.
5. In line 26, *it* (twice) refers to _____.

▶ Ask & *Answer*

Is there anything that you especially love about your country and its people? What do you think you could learn about yourself and your country by being abroad?

Address: http://www.worldpass.com 〉GO

"I left home to find home"

The prize-winning author Chimamanda Ngozi Adichie discovered her true identity as a Nigerian only by moving abroad. *Interview by Carl Wilkinson*

1. _____

I went to the U.S. when I was eight. My father was a professor teaching in California, so we spent the summer with him. I imagined I was going to a snow-filled place—to me overseas meant "snow"—and I was initially disappointed how similar San Diego* was to my hometown. Still, I felt very cool to have spent a summer in San Diego and did show off to
5 my friends. For about a week I faked a really bad American accent.

2. Do you remain rooted in Nigeria or are you keen to travel?

We don't generally have that culture of traveling and exploring in Nigeria. I don't have that wanderlust. But book tours do give me an opportunity to see other places. I was in Australia for two weeks recently, but I really just saw people at literary festivals and book readings where everyone is very nice to me.

10 Nigeria is the one place where I question myself the least. I lived in the U.S. for about seven years—it is a place that is very convenient and I am happy there, but I don't belong.

3. _____

I love the people. I love the average Nigerian. I love the sense of "can-do" in the face of all sorts of horrors. I love the languages. I love the way people walk and the way people dress traditionally.

15 There is an informality about the way people interact with each other and there's a casual acceptance and friendliness that you don't see outside Nigeria. You can walk into a shop and people will laugh and joke with you as if they knew you. I feel a real sense of connection with the country. I can go back to my ancestral village and walk the same dusty path that my great-grandfather probably walked on and that gives me a sense of being rooted.

4. _____

20 Before I went to live in the U.S. at the age of 19, I wasn't really concerned with the topic of identity. Leaving Nigeria made me much more aware of being Nigerian and what that meant. It also made me aware of race as a concept, because I didn't think of myself as black until I left Nigeria. I think you travel to search and come back home to find yourself there. In many ways travel becomes the process of finding. Travel is not the end point, it is the process. I'm not sure I would have this strong sense of being Nigerian if I had not left Nigeria.

25 **5.** _____

Yes, I went to South Africa** in 2002 and that trip changed me. I don't think I enjoyed it; I found it interesting. I found it a very strange and troubling country. Cape Town felt surreal: I didn't feel like I was in Africa, it feels more like a Mediterranean city. I felt I didn't believe the people in South Africa, that they were too ready to put on a happy face. Knowing quite a bit about South African history, I didn't buy this idea that what had taken years to set up had changed
30 in a year and now everything was fine. I wanted to write about it for a long time but I couldn't because I haven't quite sorted out the mix of feelings I had being there.

6. _____

I still don't have that drive to travel, but what I'd really like to do is go to every country in Africa. I'd also like to go back to Australia without having to do a book tour. I'd like to go back and do my own thing. I'd like to see the Aboriginal
35 communities. I wonder what it would be like to be an African tourist in Australia.

*   *San Diego: a city in Southern California where it is warm most of the year*
**   *South Africa: an African country that was ruled by a white minority for many years, and where people of different races were separated*

from *The Guardian* http://observer.guardian.co.uk/travel/story/0,6903,1431391,00.html

A Read this article submitted by a student in response to the newspaper ad. The editor has marked it with correction symbols that indicate the type of mistake made. Correct the errors.

Sp	spelling	VT	verb tense
WF	word form	WW	wrong word
P	punctuation	WO	word order
X	word(s) missing	??	I don't understand this

What was your best travel experience—or your worst? The International Institute's student newsletter wants your articles! Write about 200 words and include a photo if you can. The best articles will appear in next month's special Travel Issue.

Last year, my friend and I went on a backpacking trip in the Sierra Nevada Mountains in California. We planned to hike the John Muir
P
Trail which runs 150 miles through the mountians. We knew that
Sp
VT
the scenery will be fantastic, but we never expected to meet a fascinating character.

VT
We have saved up our money for months to buy equipment.
Sp
I bought a new sleping bag, tent, and lots of camping gadgets. But we brought too much with us, and our packs were heavy and uncomfortable.

On our third day on the trail, we met an elderly man who was walking along. His name was Bernie. He told us that
WF
his backpack was from his army days as a young man—fifty year
X
ago! We had fancy tent. He slept under a tree. We cooked on a portable camping stove. He heated his food over a fire. And if a bear
WW
came too close, he said, he just through rocks at it. At 78 years old,
??
he was finishing his twice hike of the trail.

No matter how beautiful the place you visit, it's your firsthand encounters with people that you'll remember the most. I learned something important from Bernie: to have a wonderful trip,
Sp **WO**
atttitude is more much important than money.   (212 words)

Writing an article

An article for a newsletter or magazine should inform and entertain the reader. It should include an introduction to attract the reader's interest, one or more paragraphs to form the body of the article, and a conclusion that pulls the article together.

B Write a similar article about your own best (or worst) travel experience. Include an introduction, one or more paragraphs to form the body of the article, and a conclusion.

C Pair work. Exchange papers. Mark any mistakes you see on your partner's paper with correction symbols from the box above. Give your partner other suggestions for improving the article.

4 COMMUNICATION

Activity 1: Lost at sea

A   Pair work. Read the true story below. Then with a partner, take turns describing what happened to Maralyn and Maurice Bailey using your own words.

THE BAILEYS' TRAVELS

In the early 1970s, a young British couple named Maralyn and Maurice Bailey decided to move to New Zealand. Rather than flying to their destination, the couple chose instead to start their new lives by sailing from England to New Zealand aboard their yacht Auralyn. Though Maralyn had never learned to swim and Maurice's knowledge about long-distance sailing came primarily from books, the couple was certain their trip would be a success, and set off enthusiastically in June of 1972.

Several months into the voyage, just after the couple had passed through the Panama Canal, the Auralyn came into contact with a whaling ship. A few hours later, the Auralyn was struck by an injured whale. The blow from the animal created a large hole in the yacht. With the boat sinking fast, Maralyn and Maurice inflated two rubber life rafts and roped them together. Amidst much chaos and confusion, the couple managed to get off the sinking yacht and onto the life rafts with some food, water, and a few other items.

For the first week or so, Maralyn and Maurice drank rainwater and ate the food they'd brought from their boat. Within a couple of weeks, though, the food was gone. To survive, the couple caught fish and ate them raw.

Weeks passed . . . and then months. The couple drifted on the Pacific Ocean, uncertain of where they were. By day 117, the couple's raft had become very worn. Their skin was badly sunburned and both were so exhausted that they could hardly move. And then, as the couple drifted in and out of sleep on the afternoon of day 117, Maurice thought that he saw a small black dot in the distance . . .

B   Pair work. Discuss the questions with your partner.

1. If you were in the Baileys' situation, is there anything you would've done differently? Give reasons.
2. When the yacht was first struck by the whale, how do you think the Baileys must've felt? How about after a week on the rubber raft? After two months?
3. How do you think this story ends? What do you think might have happened to Maralyn and Maurice? Find out what really happened on page 168.

Activity 2: The top three

A   Pair work. Discuss the questions below and come up with three answers for each one.

> **Real English**
> commune with nature =
> be close to nature

In your opinion, what are the top three . . .

- ways to avoid jet lag?
- most romantic cities in the world?
- local hangouts in your city?
- souvenirs you can give from your city?
- ways to occupy your time on a long car or bus trip?
- places to commune with nature?

B   Group work. Join another pair and compare ideas. As a group, come up with one final list of three for each category. Share your ideas with the class.

 Check out the CNN® video.   **Practice your English online at elt.thomson.com/worldpass**

Unit 2: The World Awaits You

A Complete these sentences about airplane flights with an appropriate verb from the box.

caught	missed	delayed	canceled
got in	diverted	called	

1. I had very bad luck getting here. I _____ my flight because traffic was so heavy on the way to the airport, and I had to wait hours for another flight.
2. The flight was _____ due to bad weather. We sat waiting in the departure lounge until the storm passed.
3. After the business meetings finished, Mr. Pak _____ the last flight back to Los Angeles and arrived home there at 11 P.M.
4. The airline agent _____ the flight to Bogotá and asked all the passengers to proceed to the gate.
5. When I found out that my flight was _____, I had to make a new reservation immediately to get home as soon as possible.
6. I'm really tired today. I came back from my vacation last night and my flight _____ at midnight!
7. Because of heavy snow at the Chicago airport, the flight was _____ to another airport, and the passengers had to go to Chicago by bus.

B Match the sentence parts to make questions that a guest would ask in a hotel.

1. Could I have a wake-up call ___
2. Could you please call a taxi ___
3. Is breakfast ___
4. Could you please send ___
5. Could you put this meal ___
6. Can I reserve ___
7. What time does ___
8. Is the hotel full ___
9. Do you have ___
10. Do you allow ___

a. included in the price?
b. all next week?
c. on my room bill, please?
d. any nonsmoking rooms?
e. the restaurant open?
f. at 7 A.M. tomorrow?
g. to take me to the airport?
h. pets in the hotel?
i. a room for next Friday?
j. someone to fix the shower?

There's an old saying . . . *A journey of a thousand miles begins with a single step.*

Even the biggest and most overwhelming project starts out with small, simple actions. We say this to encourage someone who is facing a difficult task.

"I want to change careers, but it seems so hard."

"Well, *a journey of a thousand miles begins with a single step.* Maybe you could start reading the job ads in the newspaper."

abroad
Abroad is an adverb, not a noun. It never has a preposition before it.

I hope to travel abroad after I graduate from the university.
My brother lived abroad for many years.
I hope to travel to abroad after I graduate from the university.
My brother lived in abroad for many years.

C Study the phrases in the box and complete the sentences with the correct form of the expression.

> **Word combinations with *passport***
>
> | | |
> |---|---|
> | apply for a passport | an expired passport |
> | renew a passport | show your passport |
> | stamp a passport | check a passport |
> | a valid passport | |

1. The officer _____ my passport with red ink and wrote some numbers in it.
2. Please _____ passport and ticket to the agent before boarding the ferry.
3. I'm taking my children with me on a trip to Mexico, so I need to _____ passports for them.
4. To enter the country, all travelers need to have _____ passport and a visa.
5. They wouldn't let me get on the plane because I had _____ passport. I forgot to look at the date!
6. In this country, we need to _____ our passports every ten years.
7. The police have the right to _____ your passport at any time, so you should always carry it with you when you leave your hotel.

D English has many idioms that contain comparisons. Complete each sentence with a word from the box, using your dictionary as necessary.

> | | | | | |
> |---|---|---|---|---|
> | an ox | a feather | a beet | night | nails |
> | a bat | a mouse | a bee | a bone | snow |

1. Jeff is as blind as _____ without his glasses. He can't see anything.
2. My roommate is as strong as _____. He lifts weights in the gym every day.
3. My new laptop weighs less than one kilo. It's as light as _____.
4. When I get embarrassed, my face always turns as red as _____.
5. The curtains were closed, and inside the room it was as black as _____.
6. My little sister was as quiet as _____ all evening. She didn't say a single word.
7. It hadn't rained in a month, and the soil was as dry as _____.
8. The newly painted walls of the house were as white as _____.
9. Even though she's 80 years old, my grandmother is still as busy as _____.
10. My boss doesn't care about other people's feelings. She's as hard as _____.

> ### In Other Words
>
> A traveler is anyone who takes a trip, for any purpose: *The day before the holiday, the airport was crowded with travelers.*
> A tourist is someone who is traveling for pleasure: *Tourists in my city like to visit the National Museum and the city market.*
> A passenger is someone who is traveling by plane, train, bus, etc.: *The bus driver asked the passengers to be seated.*
> A motorist is someone who is driving a car: *Police warned motorists to drive carefully during the snowstorm.*
>
> ---
>
> Drive can be a transitive verb: *I drive my car to work every morning.* It can also be intransitive: *Every morning, thousands of cars, buses, and trucks drive on the Metro Expressway into the city.*
> Sail is used for boats and ships: *The Titanic was sailing to New York when it hit an iceberg and sank.*
> Travel is used for trains (as well as cars/trucks/buses): *The new high-speed train travels at over 200 km per hour.*

1 VOCABULARY FOCUS

My first year at college

WARM UP

What's the scariest thing about going away to college?
What's the most exciting thing about it?

Real English
ace (something) =
(informal) do really well
it seems like a blur = it happened so
fast I don't remember the details

A Pair work. **These three students are going away to college next week. How do they feel about leaving home? What are their concerns? Who do you think will be happiest at school?**

Jamal

Andrea

Sarah

"We're driving up to school tomorrow and I can't wait to get away from home. It's only four hours from my house, but I'll be on my own for the first time. You probably won't want to come over for dinner—I'm a terrible cook, but my mom has said I can come home for meals on weekends if I need to. I don't know about that, but I may need her help with my laundry . . . at least at first."

"I'm apprehensive about leaving home. Since this will be my first extended period away, I know my parents are worried too. This will be a good opportunity for me to learn to be independent. One thing's for sure: I'm definitely going to sign up for as many afternoon classes as I can. I'm not an early riser!"

"This is embarrassing to admit, but I couldn't think of anything better to do, so I applied to this school. I don't have any expectations, really. I am worried about missing my friends and my boyfriend, though. I spent three weeks at a summer camp last year and I was homesick the whole time. I just hope I can make some new friends."

B Now read about how Jamal, Andrea, and Sarah feel at the end of their first term. How do they feel now?

Jamal: School has been harder than I thought. Between my part-time job, my studies, and everything else, I'm feeling overwhelmed. On top of it all, I'm getting a C minus in my macroeconomics class, which unfortunately is compulsory. I've been thinking about dropping out of school entirely and moving back home. I don't want to make a rash decision, so I'm going to think it over.

Andrea: The first term has gone so quickly—it all seems like a blur. My only mishap was during the first week of school—the battery in my wheelchair ran out on the way to class! Other than that, I've coped with university life pretty well. I aced all my final exams and I've really bonded with my three roommates. We're planning on getting an apartment together off campus next year. I can't wait!

(handwritten: TO DEAL   BAD LUCKY)

(handwritten: close CONNECTION)

Sarah: This week I'm suffering from sleep deprivation because I've been up all night studying for final exams. It's also been a challenge trying to make a budget and stick to it. That's the worst part, though. The rest of my life is awesome. I have a hectic schedule, but I live in the center of the city—so, who can complain? Best of all, I have a new boyfriend!

C Group work. **Work in groups of three. Each student should take the role of Jamal, Andrea, or Sarah. Interview each other about your college experience. Try to use the new vocabulary from A and B.**

Vocabulary Builder ▲ ----------------------------

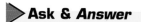

▶ Ask & Answer

Look back at Jamal's, Andrea's, and Sarah's comments in B. What advice would you give each of them at this point? Why?

A. Pair work. Look at these pairs of words. What does each word mean? Explain how the words in each pair are different from one another.

accept / except   passed / past   lose / loose

advice / advise   affect / effect

B. Choose the best answer to complete each sentence.

1. I was accepted / excepted to Coe College.
2. We meet every day accept / except Tuesday.
3. I've spent the passed / past week studying.
4. What a relief! I passed / past the test.
5. My tooth is lose / loose.

6. Don't lose / loose your student ID card.
7. My teacher gave me some good advice / advise.
8. I strongly advice / advise you to take that class.
9. Her bad attitude is affecting / effecting her grades.
10. Failing that class had a terrible affect / effect on him.

2 LISTENING
School lunches

A Listen to each person talking about school lunches. Complete the chart. (CD Tracks 07 & 08)

Name	Where from?	Where now?	Name	Where from?	Where now?
1. Jae Soo	KOREA	USA	3. Ivan	UKRAINE	SWITZ
2. Annette	NORWAY	London	4. Vanessa	PORTO RICO	

B Listen again. How does each person feel about these things? Circle *positive* or *negative*. (CD Track 09)

1. Jae Soo	a. his school lunches where he grew up Details: _____ b. school lunches where he is now Details: _____	positive negative positive negative
2. Annette	a. her school lunches growing up Details: _____ b. her daughter's school lunches now Details: _____	positive negative positive negative
3. Ivan	a. his school lunches where he grew up Details: _____ b. school lunches where he lives now Details: _____	positive negative positive negative
4. Vanessa	a. her school lunches growing up Details: _____ b. her children's school lunches now Details: _____	positive negative positive negative

C Listen again. Make notes in B about what words told you that people did or didn't like their lunches. Write the details. (CD Track 10)

▶ Ask & Answer

What did you eat most often for lunch when you were in school? What did you least enjoy eating? Did you ever share your lunch with others?

Lesson A • School life   **27**

3 LANGUAGE FOCUS

Hope and *wish*

A Pair work. **Study this cartoon. Notice the use of** *hope* **and** *wish*.

> ## Using *hope* and *wish*
>
> Use *hope* for desires or expectations that are real, probable, or possible but the outcome is uncertain. Use *wish* for desires or expectations that are unreal, unlikely, or improbable.

B The chart below explains the different uses of *hope* and *wish*. **Complete the chart with the sentences from A.**

Uses of *hope* and *wish*	Examples
Use *hope* + simple present to describe a present or future desire or expectation. Use *hope* + *will* for future expectations only.	I HOPE YOU GET AN "A"
Use *wish* + *would* + base form to express annoyance or dissatisfaction with a situation in the present or future.	*I wish it would stop raining.*
Use *wish* + simple past / past continuous to express desire for a change in a present situation. *I wish = It would be nice if . . .*	*I wish (that) I had a lot of money.* *I wish (that) it weren't raining right now.*
Use *wish* + *could* / *would* + base form to express desire for a different situation in the future.	I WISH I COULD DO BETTER
Use *wish* + past perfect to express regret about a past situation.	I wish I'D STUDIED HARDER

C Lana is not able to study for her exams because of the disruptions in her apartment. **What do you think she would think or say about the situation? Look at the picture and make sentences with** *I wish . . . would . . .*

1. I wish that bird . . . ~~STOP~~ ~~SINGING~~ WOULD STOP SINGING
2. I WISH MY SISTER WOULD TURN OFF THE TV
3. I WISH MY BROTHER WOULD ARRIVE LATELY
4. I WISH SOMEONE WOULD HANG UP THE PHONE
5. I WISH MY CAT WOULD LET ME STUDY

D Rewrite these sentences using *I wish* and the words in parentheses.

1. My sister's failing chemistry. (study) _I WISH THAT MY SISTER WOULD STUDY MORE chemistry._
2. I want to travel to Rome. (visit) _I WISH I WOULD VISIT ROME_
3. My tuition is expensive. (cheaper) _I WISH MY TUITION WOULD BE CHEAPER_
4. I didn't meet anyone at school last year. (make friends) _I WISH I WOULD make FRIENDS_
5. I can't speak Italian. (speak) _I WISH I COULD SPEAK ITALIAN_
6. I have a headache. (have aspirin) _I WISH I COULD HAVE ASPIRIN_

E Complete these sentences with the correct form of *hope* or *wish*.

1. I have a big exam tomorrow. I __HOPE__ I pass.
2. Jake didn't apply for a scholarship. Now he __WISH__ he had.
3. I __HOPE__ you have a good time at the party.
4. She went to Yale, but she __WISH__ she'd gone to Harvard.
5. That baby has been crying for an hour. I __WISH__ it would be quiet!
6. There's a woman with a baby behind us. I __WISH__ it doesn't cry during the movie.
7. I __HOPE__ I will see you at least once over the summer break.
8. I __WISH__ I hadn't lost my keys. Now I can't get into my apartment.
   I __HOPE__ I find them soon.
9. We got into an argument and I said something rude to her.
   Now I __WISH__ I hadn't. I __WISH__ I could take it all back.

F Pair work. **Role-play the situation below. Switch roles and do the role play again.**

Student A: Imagine that you are finishing your first term at college. Things are not going so well. You're bored with your classes and your grades are not good. Talk to your partner about your situation. Use *hope* and *wish* with words or phrases from the box.

Student B: Listen to your partner's problem and give him or her some advice. Use the words or phrases in the box or your own ideas.

stick it out	take a year off	cope	transfer to another school	change your major
apprehensive	drop out	hectic	quit school and find a job	

Grammar X-TRA ▶ *Make, allow,* and *let*

Read the sentences in the box. Then answer the questions below.

> They **made** us wear our uniforms during soccer practice.
> They **allowed** us to wear our uniforms during soccer practice.
> They **let** us wear our uniforms during soccer practice.

1. What do the sentences mean? How are they similar or different in meaning?
2. Using the same verbs, try to rewrite the sentences in the passive. Which one cannot be rewritten?

Pair work. **Tell your partner about the rules from a school you went to in the past. What were they like? Did you or anyone else ever break any of those rules?**

4 SPEAKING

That's an interesting question.

A Pair work. What are some situations in which people are interviewed in English?
Have you, or someone you know, ever been interviewed in English? What happened?

B Pair work. Read these general tips about what to do before, during, and after an interview.
Add your own ideas to the list. Compare your ideas with a partner.

Before an interview	During an interview	After an interview
• Get plenty of sleep the night before. • Make a list of some questions that you want to ask about the position or opportunity. • _____ • _____	• Avoid answering questions with a simple *yes* or *no* answer. • Don't rush to speak before gathering your thoughts. • _____ • _____	• Clarify what you should do next. • Shake hands with the interviewer and thank him or her. • _____ • _____

C Pair work. Read the announcement below. With your partner, prepare a list of interview questions for a candidate applying for The One World Foundation Scholarship. Include questions covering personal information, education, and language-learning experience. Add other questions of your own.

ONEWORLD

Promoting Global Understanding Through Language Study

The One World Foundation announces three scholarships of $20,000 each for learners of all ages to study English overseas in the country of their choice. Scholarships will be awarded on the basis of motivation, achievement in language study, and interest in world cultures. To apply, complete the form at www.oneworld.org. You will be contacted for an interview.

D Pair work. Take turns role-playing an interviewer for The One World Foundation and a candidate applying for the scholarship. The candidate should try to include some of the expressions in the box.

E Class work. With the class, discuss how your interview went. Did you have any problems? What strategies did you use to overcome those problems?

Interviewing phrases

Getting time to think
That's an interesting question.
Let me think about that a moment.
Just so that I understand, what you're asking is . . .

Rephrasing your answer
What I meant was . . .
What I'm trying to say is . . .
Let me put it another way.

Asking for clarification of a question
What do you mean by . . . ?
When you asked . . . , did you mean . . . ?
Are you asking about . . . ?

30   Unit 3 • School and Beyond

UNIT 3

School and Beyond

Lesson B | New school, old school

1 GET READY TO READ

School days

 How would you rate the quality of public education in your country? What could be done to improve it?

A Pair work. **Look at the illustrations below. How are these two classrooms different? Which would you rather be in? Why?**

B Pair work. **Think about your experiences in high school. Which of the statements below describe what your education was like? Check (✓) your answers. Then compare and discuss your answers with a partner.**

	Usually	Sometimes	Hardly ever
1. Teachers were strict.		✓	
2. We had a lot of tests.		✓	
3. We went on field trips to learn more about a subject.		✓	
4. Classes featured drills and memorization of facts.			✓
5. Most classes had no more than twenty students.			✓
6. Classes were engaging; I looked forward to going.		✓	
7. Students worked on projects in groups.		✓	
8. Students got practical, hands-on experience outside the classroom.			✓
9. Classes in art and sports were offered.	✓		
10. Other: _____			

▶ **Ask & Answer**

Was your high school experience mostly positive or negative? Do you think your education prepared you for your future? Why or why not?

A Pair work. **Read the online discussion between Yoon-Hee and Gordon on page 33, and underline the ideas you agree with. Then compare your answers with a partner.**

B **Read the online discussion again. Which writer would agree with the following statements? Circle the correct answer.**

1. There should be less emphasis in schools on drilling and taking tests.   ⟨Yoon-Hee⟩   Gordon   both

2. Schools need to promote critical thinking and develop skills that students can use in the real world.   Yoon-Hee   Gordon   ⟨both⟩

3. Giving students the chance to get more hands-on experience is a nice idea, but in the real world it's too difficult to do.   Yoon-Hee   ⟨Gordon⟩   both

4. Students need to spend more time memorizing certain things in school.   Yoon-Hee   ⟨Gordon⟩   both

5. Courses such as music, art, and cooking should be added to a school's standard curriculum.   ⟨Yoon-Hee⟩   Gordon   both

6. The main reason we go to school is to learn science, math, reading, and writing.   Yoon-Hee   ⟨Gordon⟩   both

C **Complete the sentences below with the correct word or phrase.**

1. Many families in Korea spend a lot of money to send their children to _____ so that they can _____ .

2. _____ believed that knowing how to _____, _____, and plant a garden were as important as studying _____ and science.

3. Many schools today have a minimum of _____ students in every classroom.

4. In a recent *National Geographic* article, only _____ % of people aged _____- _____ were able to find _____ on a map.

5. According to Gordon, too many of today's high school graduates are unable to _____ or _____ .

D **Find the words in the reading. Then circle the word or phrase each is most similar to.**

1. In line 1, *foster* is most similar in meaning to promote / discourage.
2. In line 12, *apply* is most similar in meaning to abandon / utilize.
3. In line 20, *cultivate* is most similar in meaning to develop / neglect.
4. In line 26, *goofing off* is most similar in meaning to studying seriously / playing around.
5. In line 31, *coherent* is most similar in meaning to logical / confusing.
6. In line 35, *a solid foundation* is most similar in meaning to a good knowledge / passing grades.

The Globe
Our Readers Respond | Last week, we asked readers how they would improve the overall quality of education where they live. We received responses from all over the world.

Instead of being institutions that foster critical thinking and address the real-world needs of students, many of today's schools are more like "information factories"–places where we memorize as much data as we can (most of which we later forget) so that we can "pass a test." In my country, for example, one's future–from the major you will study to the job you will eventually get–often depends on whether or not you pass the test to get into a good
5 college. Families spend enormous amounts of money to send their kids to cram schools to help them prepare for and pass the university entrance exam. Your education becomes focused on this one single goal: passing the test.

In my opinion, if we want to talk about improving the quality of education for all, the first thing we should do is to place less emphasis on rote memorization and test-taking in our schools and more emphasis on developing critical thinking and important life skills. Classes in all grades should feature more hands-on, practical learning.
10 Let's take one example. We've all studied science from a book. But students can also learn about it by going on field trips and spending time in nature, or volunteering at a local wildlife preserve. "Learning by doing" is a great way to develop practical skills and to apply what we've learned in books. Many high school and university graduates often wish they'd had a chance to do more of this kind of learning in school. I wish I had!

We also need to understand that being educated is about more than studying science, math, and languages. Of
15 course these subjects are important. But so are painting and music. And what about learning how to cook, plant a garden, and make your own clothes? Mahatma Gandhi himself believed that these skills were just as important as science and math and belonged in every school curriculum. I couldn't agree more.
— Yoon-Hee Pak   Seoul, Korea

I'm writing to respond to Yoon-Hee Pak's comment. First off, I would say that I agree with her that schools should
20 be places that cultivate critical thinking and prepare students to meet the challenges they will face in the real world.

On a philosophical level, I also think it would be great if our classrooms featured more hands-on learning. But let's be realistic. Many private and public schools around the world, from elementary school on up, have a minimum of forty students in a classroom. Ms. Pak talks about spending time in nature rather than learning science from a book. It's a lovely idea, and in a perfect world, classroom ratio would be ten students for every
25 one teacher. But with forty or more students, how can a teacher make sure the students are learning, and not just goofing off while they're "out in nature" or volunteering somewhere?

At the start of her letter, Ms. Pak says that schools ought to spend less time on drills and tests. In my opinion, students need to spend *more* time drilling and memorizing certain information. I say this because in a recent *National Geographic* study, only about 25% of the 18-24-year-olds interviewed from around the world were able
30 to identify countries such as Israel and Iran correctly on a map! An alarming number of high school graduates today can't do basic math or write a coherent essay. How are people like this supposed to compete in the job market?

I guess the question for me is why do we go to school? Is it to go on field trips? To learn how to paint or sew clothes? I don't think so. We do so to master academic skills in core areas such as reading, writing, mathematics,
35 and science. Our schools need to be doing more to make sure that all students are graduating with a solid foundation in these subjects. If that means more drills and tests, well then, so be it.
— Gordon Pickering   Canberra, Australia

▶ **Ask & *Answer***

Whose point of view–Yoon-Hee's or Gordon's–do you agree with? Why? If you were going to send a response to *The Globe* about improving the overall quality of education where you live, what would you suggest?

Real English
so be it =
it should be that way

3 WRITING
Writing an opinion essay

A Do coed classes work better for boys and girls or should they be taught in separate classes? On a separate piece of paper make a list of the advantages and disadvantages of coed classes.

B Read this student's essay about coed schools and answer these questions.

1. What is the thesis statement of the essay?
2. What topic is discussed in paragraph 2? What examples are given?
3. What topic is discussed in paragraph 3? What examples are given?
4. What is the writer's opinion about coed schools?

Using a thesis statement

A thesis statement tells the reader the focus of your essay and what it's going to be about.

Essay

What are some of the advantages and disadvantages of coeducational schools? In your opinion, which are more important —the advantages or the disadvantages? Write about 250 words.

Until twenty years ago, coeducational schools were not common in my country. The modernization of our educational system means that now more boys and girls are going to school together. Attending a coed school has both advantages and disadvantages.

Coeducational schools have several important benefits. For one thing, students at these schools are better prepared for life after graduation. In the working world, we interact every day with both men and women, as supervisors, colleagues, and customers. Furthermore, diversity inside a school is very positive, not just as a preparation for work. There is much to be learned from contact with members of the opposite sex, because they may act and think differently from ourselves. And most importantly, coeducational schools are fair for everyone. All students, male and female, have access to the same teachers, courses, and opportunities.

Of course, there are also disadvantages of boys and girls studying together. Teachers and parents say that students are distracted by the presence of the opposite sex in the classroom. This can make it more difficult to concentrate on studying. A more serious problem with coed schools is that they can build stereotypes. Boys may not want to study art or music when girls are there, and girls may feel pressure to keep quiet in science classes.

In my opinion, though, the benefits far outweigh the disadvantages. Coeducational schools better prepare young people for the future, and at the same time, allow them to have a more enjoyable social life.

C Should students in secondary and high school wear uniforms? On a separate piece of paper make a list of the advantages and disadvantages of school uniforms.

D Use your list to write an essay of about 250 words answering the questions below.

What are some of the advantages and disadvantages of school uniforms?
In your opinion, should students be able to choose what to wear to school?

E Pair work. Exchange papers with a partner and make suggestions on how to improve your partner's essay.

4 COMMUNICATION

Activity 1: One-day workshop

A Pair work. **Read the brochure to the right. What kind of workshop is being offered? Would you pay to attend? Why or why not?**

Do you wish that you could take photos like a pro?

Join a Saturday workshop and cultivate your inner vision!

B Pair work. **You and your partner are going to design a one-day workshop. Choose a workshop type from the box below or create your own. Then discuss these questions.**

1. By the end of the workshop, what should attendees be able to do?
2. What hours will the workshop be held? What are people going to do during different times? Design the course schedule. List specifics.
3. Who is going to be leading the workshop? Will you have guest speakers?
4. Do attendees need to have any experience or to bring anything to the workshop?
5. How many people in total can join the workshop?
6. What is the cost to attend?

This one-day workshop emphasises hands-on learning. The morning hours are dedicated to exploring different subjects (human, natural settings, architecture, and others) and presenting various techniques, such as choice of camera, using natural light, and working with props. Attendees spend the afternoon in the field applying what they've learned.

Every Saturday from 9:00-6:00

Cost: $300
Experience: None required
Maximum class size: 10
Instructor(s): Award-winning photographers Elizabeth Yee, Anthony Parker, Satoru Watanabe, Juana Sandoval

Possible workshops

How to . . .
- find the perfect job
- date and find true love
- start your own online business
- think like a millionaire and make more money
- dance like a pro
- make the perfect meal
- master the art of calligraphy
- make and market your own movies
- look like a model
- speak [*name of language*] fluently

C Pair work. **Using the information you discussed in B, design a simple brochure describing your workshop.**

D Group work. **Share your brochure and workshop schedule with at least four other pairs in your class. Answer their questions. Take notes about their workshops.**

E Pair work. **Choose one of the workshops to attend. Explain your choice to a partner.**

Activity 2: Seven wishes and three hopes

Pair work. **Complete the following seven wishes and three hopes with your own ideas. Then compare them with a partner.**

I wish I had . . .   I wish I wasn't/weren't . . .   I wish I could . . .   I wish I was/were . . .   I hope my teacher . . .
I wish I hadn't . . .   I wish I knew . . .   I wish I didn't . . .   I hope the world . . .   I hope my family . . .

 Check out the CNN® video. **Practice your English online at elt.thomson.com/worldpass**

Unit 3: School and Beyond

A Match the university courses with the topics they include.

1. agriculture ___
2. political science ___
3. anthropology ___
4. psychology ___
5. engineering ___
6. accounting ___
7. zoology ___
8. environmental studies ___
9. economics ___
10. physics ___

a. the science of heat, energy, and light
b. how the governments of different countries operate
c. what causes prices to increase
d. designing and building machines, roads, bridges, etc.
e. the causes and effects of pollution
f. recording the income and expenses of a business
g. different types of animals and their bodies
h. similarities and differences in cultures
i. how to raise farm animals and plants
j. the human mind and how it works

B How did you do on the exam? Write the answers in the correct box, then circle the informal answers.

> Don't ask!   I aced it.   I passed.   I failed.
> I flunked.   I did well.   I bombed.   I did very poorly.

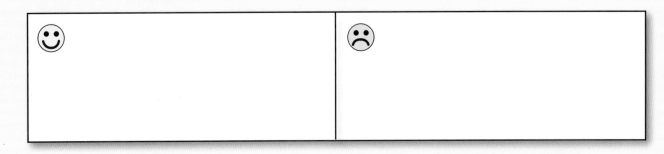

I didn't know that!
The word *educate* comes from a Latin verb that means "lead out." It was believed that teachers led students out of their own world and into the world of knowledge.

C Where will these people study? Fill in the name of the institution, using your dictionary as necessary.

> technical college   medical school   seminary   art academy
> dental school   university   military academy   law school

1. Alex wants to become a minister in his church. _____
2. Larissa would like to work as a lawyer for immigrants. _____
3. Omar hopes to become a doctor and work with children. _____
4. Brenda wants to study painting and drawing. _____
5. José is planning to study European history and politics. _____
6. Rosela wants to learn how to repair computers. _____
7. Young-Mi wants to help people keep their teeth healthy. _____
8. Dan intends to become an officer in his country's army. _____

Expansion Pages

D Match these phrases with their meanings.

> **Word combinations with *education***
>
> 1. get an education ___
> 2. pay for an education ___
> 3. primary education ___
> 4. secondary education ___
> 5. higher education ___
> 6. the standard of education ___
> 7. adult education ___
> 8. physical education ___
>
> a. college and university
> b. high school
> c. go to school and complete your studies
> d. classes for older students
> e. classes in sports and exercise
> f. elementary school
> g. the usual level of studies
> h. give money for school tuition

E Use a form of one of the phrases from D to complete the sentences.

1. Many students in my country hope to go to foreign universities, because access to _____ here is very limited.
2. I want to work in _____ after I graduate, because I love to work with young children.
3. I never enjoyed my _____ classes in school, because I'm not very good at sports.
4. _____ in this country is coeducational. Boys and girls attend high school together.
5. My brother got a job to help _____. Tuition, books, and fees are very expensive here.
6. My mother really enjoys taking _____ courses at the community center. She's taken painting, French, and computer classes.
7. The _____ in my country is very high. Nearly everyone graduates from high school, and many students go on to university.
8. If girls in developing countries can _____, they are better prepared to get a job and help support their families.

> **In Other Words**
>
> A class is a period of teaching: *I have English class three times a week.*
> A lesson is a period of teaching a skill: *I've been taking tennis/cooking lessons on Saturdays.*
> In British English, lesson is used with a meaning similar to class: *Our math lesson is at 10:00 every day.*
> A course is a series of classes in a particular subject: *I'm taking a course in women's history.*
> A major is the main subject you study at a college or university: *Last year I changed my major from biology to environmental science.*
>
> ---
>
> Teacher is the most general term: *Ms. Diaz is my science/Spanish/drawing teacher.*
> A professor is a college or university teacher: *Dr. Yun is a professor of history at National University.*
> An instructor teaches a practical or physical skill: *My driving instructor is very patient with me!*
> A tutor gives private lessons: *The tutor comes to our house to give my son English lessons after school.*

> faculty
> **Faculty** is a collective noun that refers to all the teachers in a particular academic program:
>> *Dr. Jones is a member of the faculty of the College of Agriculture.*
> It does not mean the academic program itself:
>> *I am a student in the faculty of medicine.*
>> *I am a student in the College of Medicine.*

Review: Units 1–3

1 LANGUAGE CHECK

There is a mistake in one of the underlined parts of each sentence. Rewrite the incorrect word or phrase correctly.
Some sentences have no mistakes. Write OK next to them.

1. I really wish I haven't spent all my money on those shoes yesterday. _____hadn't spent_____
2. We were such disappointed to hear about the closing of the old theater. _____
3. When you didn't answer the phone, I knew you should have gone out. _____
4. I could have bought the movie tickets last week, but I decided to wait. _____
5. We should have remember to stop the mail delivery before our vacation. _____
6. It's such an important book that everyone should read it. _____
7. I hope I'd get time off from work so that I can take a vacation. _____
8. I was completely amazing to see that I had gotten 100% on my quiz. _____
9. My best friend got married, but now she wishes she is still single. _____
10. Don't you wish you had practiced more before your driving test? _____
11. Johan hopes he had spent more time with his kids when they were little. _____
12. I wish I didn't had to get up so early every morning to go to class. _____
13. My parents let us do our homework every night before we could watch TV. _____
14. The soup was so spicy as I couldn't eat much of it. _____
15. We shouldn't have taken the kids to see such a shocked movie. _____

2 VOCABULARY CHECK

Read this summary and change and/or add to the word in parentheses to form an appropriate new word or
phrase that fits in the context.

Last night, I watched a TV interview with Dexter Marshall, the director of the new movie *Dead and Gone*. He said
he was (1. bore) _____bored with_____ making Hollywood-style blockbuster movies, so he decided to shoot an old-fashioned
detective movie in black and white. It's a very (2. disturb) _____ story, about the murder of an old man. It was
(3. relative) _____ easy for him to find people to work on the movie. In fact, a lot of the actors are household
names, and the cast really (4. bond) _____ each other while making the movie. One (5. draw) _____
_____ of this project being in black and white was that it was necessary to have special costumes made for the black-and-
white film.

Marshall had a lot of trouble finding a company that was interested in the movie. He said it was
(6. nerve) _____ trying to get a studio to give him money. They said moviegoers had a lot of
(7. expect) _____ about what a movie should be like, and this was too different. It took them months to
(8. strike a) _____ about how to produce the movie, even though Marshall had (9. first) _____
experience from making black-and-white movies before he (10. drop) _____ of film school.

In the interview, he didn't (11. give) _____ the ending of the movie though—he said it would be out
next month, and we should see for ourselves. It was really a (12. fascinate) _____ interview. I never realized
how much happens behind the scenes of a big movie.

3 NOW YOU'RE TALKING!

Situation 2

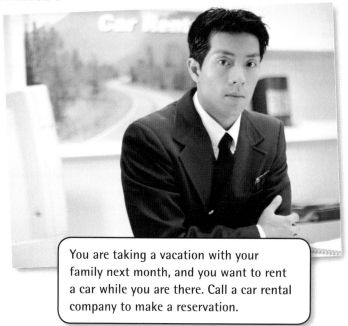

You are taking a vacation with your family next month, and you want to rent a car while you are there. Call a car rental company to make a reservation.

You and your partner are officers of the National Association of TV Fans. Every year, the association gives the Comedy Awards for the three funniest shows on TV. Work together to choose this year's winners.

Situation 3

A Pair work. Look at the pictures and imagine what the people in each situation might say. Then briefly review the language notes from Units 1–3 on pages 154–155.

B Pair work. Role-play situations 1, 2, and 3 with a partner. Notice how well you and your partner do the role play. Ask your partner's opinion about your performance.

C Now rate your speaking. Use + for good, ✓ for OK, and – for things you need to improve. Then add two goals for the improvement of your speaking.

You want to get a part-time job as an English tutor for children. You go to a job interview with the program's director.

How did you do?	1	2	3
I was able to express my ideas.			
I spoke easily and fluently, without hesitation.			
I spoke at a good rate of speed—not too fast or too slow.			
I used new vocabulary from the units.			
I used at least three expressions from the units.			
I practiced the grammar from the units.			
Goals for improvement: 1. _____ 2. _____			

Contemporary Issues

Lesson A | In the city

1 VOCABULARY FOCUS

I can get it for free.

 What kind of music do you like to listen to? Has the way you listen to or purchase music changed in the past five years? How?

A Pair work. **Read this article about a controversy and answer the questions with a partner.**

1. What is the problem?
2. What are the two opposing viewpoints?

Recently, companies in the recording industry have begun cracking down on people who download music for free on the Internet. It made the news recently when two dozen college students were taken to court for downloading copyrighted music and movies. Their case is still pending and the outcome is uncertain. It remains to be seen whether this case will have an effect on how and where consumers get their music in the future.

Is downloading a crime? Critics argue that for years, the music industry has churned out mainstream fare that is mediocre and too expensive. Due to downloading, companies are panicking because they are losing their monopoly on music production. These large corporations are greedy, say critics, and are simply afraid of losing control.

Others argue that the artists and those who produce the products must be compensated fairly for their work. When you download music for free, you rip off the people who make the music by robbing them of their income. Supporters of this argument remind us that unauthorized copying of music is not only unethical—it's also illegal! Not all of the companies making music products are huge corporations, after all. Small companies, which often feature emerging artists, are also hurt.

B Find an expression in blue in A that means:

1. poor in quality _mediocre_
2. waiting to be decided _PENDING_
3. beginning to be known or noticed _EMERGING_
4. not officially approved _UNAUTHORIZED_
5. strictly enforcing laws ~~TAKEN TO COURT~~ _CRACKIN DOWN_
6. cheat _RIP OFF_
7. wanting more money, control, or power _GREEDY_
8. had legal action taken against _TAKE TO COURT_
9. produced quickly without attention to quality _MEDIOCRE_
10. complete control by a business or group of businesses _CHURNED OUT_
11. not morally right _UNETHICAL_
12. feeling fear and anxiety _PANICKING_
13. given payment _COMPENSATED_
14. people who buy things _CONSUMERS_

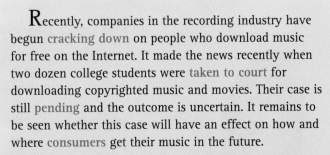

Real English
be all for (something) =
completely support an
action, idea, etc.

C Group work. **In the same article in A, there was a poll. Read the polling options below and vote for the one you agree with most. Then share your answers as a group.**

Reader's Poll: What do you think about downloading music from the Internet for free? Check the opinion you agree with.

☐ I'm against it. Downloading music from the Internet rips off the people who make the music.

☐ I think we need to compromise. Downloading music is good for emerging artists and consumers.

☐ I don't know. Downloading lets us listen to different kinds of music, but maybe we should pay something.

☐ I'm all for it. The Internet is about the free sharing of ideas.

Pair work. **Read these expressions that contain the words** *eye* **and** *see.*
Then work with a partner to use them to complete the story below.

> remains to be seen = is not certain (what will happen) have seen the light = understood something
> saw eye to eye = agreed; had the same opinion opened my eyes = made me aware of
> turned a blind eye = pretended not to notice (bad behavior) see what I can do = try to help
> wait and see = be patient

Two weeks ago I received a letter from a large record company. I was being taken to court for breaking the law. My crime? Downloading free music from the Internet!

I couldn't believe it. I'm only a college student. I've never been in trouble before. But I guess this has been a problem for a while. At first, the music industry (1) _turned a blind eye_ to the problem. Now they are doing something about it.

I met my lawyer last week. "Will I have to pay a big fine?" I asked. "I don't know," he said. "That (2) _remains to be seen_." He assured me, "I'll do my best—I'll (3) _see what I can do_." Fortunately, we all (4) _saw eye to eye_ on one thing: no one wants to see me put in jail for this! That's a relief.

Even though I'm anxious, there's nothing I can do about it now. I'll just have to (5) _wait and see_. This experience has really (6) _opened my eyes_ to the seriousness of downloading music illegally. Before I received the letter, I was unaware of it. I can also say that I finally (7) _have seen the light_ when it comes to free downloading: I'm going to stop doing it!

2 LISTENING

Our cities are growing.

A Pair work. **Read and discuss these two predictions with a partner.**
Do you think these trends are positive or negative? Why?

- According to U.N.-Habitat, 60% of the world's population will be living in cities by 2030.
- The urban population will grow from 2.86 billion to nearly five billion.

B **Listen. Two experts are being interviewed about unchecked urban growth. Which of the four statements represents the** *main* **point Fiona is trying to make? Which statement best represents Hector's opinion?** (CD Tracks 11 & 12)

1. Fiona B   a. Good planning can solve urban problems.   c. It's more violent in our cities.
2. Hector A   b. We must limit the growth of our cities.   d. A more organized transportation system is the key.

C **Listen again. Complete each statement the speaker makes.** (CD Track 13)

1. Fiona
   a. In this city, for example, there's a serious _Housing_ .
   b. This unchecked urban sprawl destroys _farmland and water sources_ for the city.
2. Hector
   a. There's widespread _poverty_ and lack of _housing_ .
   b. Since 1989, the citizens there have worked together to raise the _overall quality of life_.
   c. We can build and coordinate _bus and train system_ that don't pollute the environment as much.

▶ Ask & Answer

What issues are facing urban areas in your country? If you were an urban planner, what improvements would you suggest for your city?

3 LANGUAGE FOCUS

Past and present unreal conditionals

A Study the grammar charts. Then answer the questions below.

Present unreal conditional		
if clause	main clause	meaning
If I had a car, If I were presenting in English, If I could graduate early,	I'd be happy to drive. I might be nervous. I'd do it.	*I don't have a car.* *I will probably be presenting in Spanish.* *Graduating early is unlikely.*

improbable

Past unreal conditional		
if clause	main clause	meaning
If I had passed the test, If I had been presenting in English,	I would've been happy. I might have been nervous.	*I failed the test.* *I presented in Spanish.*

1. Which verb forms can be used in the *if* clauses? Which modal forms can be used in the main clauses?
2. Which conditional do we use to talk about present or future situations that are improbable? Which one do we use to talk about situations in the past that could have happened but didn't?

B Nick is unhappy living alone in the city. Read his letter to a friend. Underline the examples of the present unreal conditional. Circle the examples of the past unreal conditional.

Dear Ben,

Today marks one month in the city. It's been very difficult. First of all, I don't know anyone. (1) If I had some friends here, I might be happier. My new job has been disappointing, too. (2) If the work were more interesting, the job would be bearable. But I can't stand it! I don't like this part of the city either. (3) If I were living in a more exciting neighborhood, it might be interesting. Basically, everything around here closes around 7 P.M. so there's nothing to do but stay home and watch TV.

(4) If you had asked me before, I never would've predicted that living alone in the city would be this difficult. (5) If I had listened to my parents, I wouldn't have moved to the city so soon. I know that now. And my parents were also right about my finances. (6) If I hadn't been so stubborn, I could've stayed home an extra year and saved more money. At the moment, I have almost no spending money. Well, one thing's for sure, (7) if I could move home tomorrow, I'd do it!

Nick

P.S. Come and visit me. I'm lonely!

C Pair work. Look again at the numbered sentences in the letter and write *T* for true or *F* for false for the statements below. Explain your answers to a partner.

1. __T__ Nick wishes he had some friends.
2. __T__ He wishes his job were more interesting.
3. __T__ He wishes his neighborhood were more interesting.
4. __F__ He isn't surprised that living in the city is hard.
5. __F__ He wishes he hadn't taken his parents' advice.
6. __T__ He thinks he was stubborn.
7. __F__ He likes his independence in the city.

42 Unit 4 • Contemporary Issues

D Pair work. **With a partner, correct these conditional sentences so that they make sense.**

1. Class was canceled. If someone ~~told~~ [*had*] me yesterday, I wouldn't have shown up at school today.
2. If I hadn't argued with my boss, I still ~~had a job~~. *I WOULD STILL HAVE A JOB*
3. If I ~~would be doing~~ better in class, I'd be getting an A. *I were be doing...*
4. If the city ~~wouldn't be~~ so expensive, we weren't moving to the country. *weren't*

E **Read about this creative solution to a problem in London. Then rewrite the sentences that follow.**

Homework

London News—At certain subway stations in the city, there has been a problem with gang members hanging around and causing trouble. Officials have cracked down on the problem, using a creative solution. They pipe classical music loudly throughout the station, and it seems to drive away the troublemakers. Passengers feel safer and the city doesn't waste money on taking people to court.

1. Kids are bored, so they hang out in gangs.
   <u>If kids weren't bored, they wouldn't hang out in gangs.</u>
2. They skip school, so they don't get a proper education.
   If they didn't skip school, they would get a proper education.
3. They cause trouble, so the subway passengers are scared of them.
   If they didn't cause trouble, the subway passengers wouldn't be scared of them.
4. A few months ago officials piped classical music into the stations, so the problem was solved.
   If classical music weren't piped into the stations a few months ago by officials, the problem wouldn't have been solved.
5. The kids didn't like that kind of music, so they left the stations.
   If the kids liked that kind of music, they wouldn't left the stations.
6. It has been so successful that it has been copied in Australia and Canada as well.
   If it hadn't been so successful, it wouldn't have been copied...

F Pair work. **Talk to your partner about these issues in your city. Use conditionals where appropriate.**

> *If they hadn't cracked down on unauthorized street parking, the traffic problems would be worse.*

| traffic | urban sprawl | graffiti | noise |
| crime | transportation | trash pickup | gangs |

Grammar X-TRA — Low possibility

> If it **happens** to rain that day, we'll cancel the picnic.
> If it **should (happen to)** rain that day, we **might** cancel the picnic.
> If I **were to** move to France, I'd study French before I left.

> These structures are used for future conditional sentences indicating situations that probably won't happen or have a low possibility of happening.

Your friend Wally is a chronic worrier. He's going on a trip. Read his worries and answer him using a future conditional.

1. What if I miss the bus to the airport?
2. What if my flight is delayed?
3. What if I lose my passport?
4. What if I get homesick?

> *If you happen to miss the bus to the airport, I'll give you a ride.*

Without a doubt

A Pair work. *One-Minute Message* is a TV program that lets viewers speak their minds on current issues for only one minute or less. Read the interview and then discuss the questions below with a partner.

Host: Today, our topic is the proposed city law that would ban smoking in all public buildings, and our guests have a lot to say on the subject. What do you think, Andrew?

Andrew: I'm convinced that the anti-smoking law is a terrible idea. The government keeps taking away more and more of our freedom. Just wait—in a few years, they'll have a law against eating pizza or french fries because they're unhealthy, or a law against watching too much TV! Next they'll start telling us what color our houses can be, or our cars. Politicians shouldn't be allowed to interfere with our personal lives like that. The government has a lot of stupid ideas, and this is another one of them.

Host: Thanks! That's all there's time for. And our next guest is Tomas. What's your opinion?

Tomas: Without a doubt, we need this law, because it will provide cleaner air for everybody. When people smoke indoors, everybody suffers, including nonsmokers. There's a lot of research that shows that breathing other people's smoke is harmful, especially to children. Smokers say they have a right to enjoy a cigarette, and that's fine, as long as other people aren't affected. But it isn't right for smokers to pollute the air in public spaces and harm other people's health.

Host: Time's up! Thank you very much. And one more point of view, Cassie.

Cassie: I think it would be better just to ban smoking in a few places—for instance, hospitals, because they're full of sick people. But when people go to a club or restaurant, they should be able to smoke if they feel like it. Of course, smoking shouldn't be allowed in taxis, or buses. Not only that, but I really hate it when people smoke on the train, because it gives me a headache. I don't smoke, so if they passed the law, it wouldn't really be a problem for me.

1. Who do you think gave the best message?
2. What made this message effective?
3. How could the other speakers explain their opinions more effectively?

B What do you think? Mark your opinions on these issues, and make notes of your reasons.

1. Should people be allowed to purchase guns and keep them in their homes?
   ☐ Yes ☐ No ☒ Only if . . .
   Reasons: _The person made an specsic and difficult course_

2. Should city governments take steps to control urban growth?
   ☒ Yes ☐ No ☐ Only if . . .
   Reasons: _____

3. Should scientists assist women over 40 who want to have children?
   ☒ Yes ☐ No ☐ Only if . . .
   Reasons: _Everyone has the right to have children._

C Group work. In groups of four, role-play the *One-Minute Message* show using the issues in **B**. One student is the host who asks a question and times the speakers while they give their opinions. Change roles and practice again until you've covered all of the topics. Try to use some of the expressions in the box.

D Now think of an issue that is important to you and give a one-minute message about it to the whole class.

Expressing an opinion	
Stating your opinion	**Giving additional reasons**
I strongly believe . . .	*Not only that, but . . .*
I'm convinced that . . .	*Not to mention the fact that . . .*
Without a doubt, . . .	*And besides, . . .*
Illustrating your point	
For instance . . .	
Take, for example, . . .	
To give you an idea . . .	

Contemporary Issues

UNIT 4

| *Lesson B* | Conflict resolution |

1 GET READY TO READ

What's going on here?

Think of a conflict you've been involved in recently.
What was it about? How did you resolve it?

A Pair work. **The words and expressions in the box are all related to conflict. Which ones do you know?**
Look up the ones you don't know in a dictionary. Then discuss the meaning of each with a partner.

beat (someone) up	clash	combat	confront	get into a brawl
harass	intimidate	lose your temper	pick on	threaten

B Pair work. **Look at the photos and describe what is happening in each.**
Use the words and phrases from A as well as ideas of your own.

CLASH

CLASH or COMBAT
CONFRONT

C Pair work. **Discuss these questions.**

1. How do you think each conflict in the photos started?
2. What could be done to defuse or resolve each problem?
3. Do you think each situation could have been prevented? If so, how?

Lesson B • Conflict resolution   45

2 READING

Bullying—what can you do about it?

A Pair work. What do you think *bullying* means? Agree on a definition for the word with your partner and write it on the line below. Then read the first two paragraphs of the article on page 47. How does the definition of bullying compare with yours?

Bullying is the act of one person or a group of people repeatedly picking on another

B Now read about the three people on page 47 and complete the first two columns of the chart.

	How was he or she being bullied?	What did he or she do about the bullying?	Helpful in dealing with bullying?
Mayumi	The kids teased her in class and picked on her in the schoolyard	She told her mother about the bullying	Yes, Now she's been doing better in school and is making friends
Adam	Guys were calling him DORK and threatening to beat him up	fought with the bullies	No, He was suspended from school for two days total
Blanca	Brett was attacking her ideas and spreading rumors about her	Confront Brett about his behavior	Not all. Brett is just more carefully on his words

C Look at your answers in the second column in B. Did these actions help each person to deal with the bullying in some productive, helpful way? Write *yes* or *no* in the last column.

D The words and expressions in the box are all in the reading. Make sure you understand their meaning. Then complete the sentences with the correct form of each one.

> fitting in (line 16)   insecure (line 48)   opponent (line 55)   behind my back (line 65)   dreading (line 68)

1. Chee's _dreading_ the university entrance exam. He's sure he won't pass.
2. Jill is more interested in developing her own style than with _fitting in_ with the other girls.
3. Just before the match, Lynn's _opponent_ became ill, and so the game had to be rescheduled.
4. If you're angry with Marco, tell him why. Don't talk about him _behind his back_.
5. Even though Trey is a smart, outgoing person, he becomes very shy and _insecure_ whenever he has to talk in front of a group.

E Complete these sentences with the correct word or phrase from the reading.

1. In line 2, *one* refers to _Bullies_ _the action of being bullied_
2. In line 10, *Others* refers to _Victims_ _and teased_
3. In line 23, *it* refers to _"They teased her ..."_
4. In line 49, *it* refers to _Harassment_
5. In line 64, *it* refers to _"Brett became very argumentative_ _(the situation)"_

▶ Ask & Answer

What would you have done if you were in the situations featured in the reading?
What are other things people can do to stop or prevent bullying?

World Link

The problem of bullying goes beyond childhood and adolescence. At the age of thirty, people who were bullies as children are five times more likely to have been convicted of a serious crime as non-bullies.

Source: *Maine Project Against Bullying*

Bullying—
what can you do about it?

Bullies. If you haven't been the victim of one, you may know someone who has. Bullying is the act of one person or a group of people repeatedly
5 **picking on another. A bully creates an environment of fear and intimidation in order to feel powerful and in control.**

Victims of bullying often deal with different types of harassment including constant teasing, name
10 calling, or physical abuse. Others are the subject of hurtful (usually untrue) rumors.

New Kid on the Block

Mayumi Sato, 11, recently returned to Japan with her family after six years in Germany, where her
15 father was working. Now attending middle school in Tokyo, she initially had a difficult time fitting in. "Most of the kids in Mayumi's class had gone to the same schools and grown up together, so I'm not surprised that they saw my daughter as different at
20 first," says Mayumi's mother, Hiroko. "But some of the kids were just mean. They teased her in class and picked on her in the schoolyard." At first, Mayumi tried to ignore it, but then she finally told her mother what was going on. "I'm glad she came to me,"
25 Hiroko says. "You know, a lot of kids would be too embarrassed to talk about something like this. But if you're being bullied, you *do* need to talk about it—to a parent, a friend, or someone you trust—so that something can be done." Hiroko spoke to one of
30 the girl's teachers, who promised to keep an eye on Mayumi and to encourage the kids in the class to be more welcoming towards her. This approach seems to be working. "Mayumi's been doing better in school and is making friends," says Hiroko. "She's definitely
35 happier than she was those first few weeks."

On the defense

After being picked on for months by a group of older boys at the high school he goes to, Adam Wheeland, 15, had had enough. "These three guys
40 were always calling me *dork* in the hallways and threatening to beat me up. One day I came to school, and they'd glued my locker shut. They were standing nearby laughing, and I lost it. I got into a fight with one of them." Wheeland and the other boy were suspended from
45 school for two days for fighting. When they returned, the trouble continued. Wheeland realized he needed to approach the situation differently. "The thing about bullies is that they're often very insecure people. These guys who've been harassing me only do it when they're
50 together. So I try to stay in a group with my friends now. Wheeland, who is a straight-A student, has also decided he needs to do things that boost his self-confidence. He's joined the debate club and is taking a martial-arts class. "Now when I see those guys around school, I think
55 of them as the opponent in a competition. I feel less nervous, and I think they've noticed that."

Trouble at work

Thirty-year-old Blanca Montero, an up-and-coming civil engineer at Allied Systems, was assigned recently
60 to work on a team project with Brett—a colleague who had joined the company around the same time she had. Almost immediately, there were problems. "Whenever I disagreed with his ideas, Brett became very argumentative. It was really difficult," says Montero.
65 "Then he started complaining about me behind my back—you know, telling others that my work was second-rate." In a month, Montero went from loving her job to dreading every day. She finally decided to confront Brett about his behavior. "I scheduled a time to speak to him.
70 Actually, before we got together, I thought about what I was going to say so that I could stay calm during our meeting." On the day they met, Montero explained the situation to Brett. "I asked how he'd feel if I—or others on the team—attacked his ideas or spread rumors about
75 him. Though he didn't say much during our talk, he did listen and promised to work on being more considerate." So have things changed? "I've noticed that Brett is trying to be more aware of his behavior—and not just with me, but with others on the team, too. Things aren't perfect,"
80 says Montero, "but I'm glad we spoke. If we hadn't, I suspect I would've lost my temper at some point or quit the project."

3 WRITING

Expressing an opinion in a short message

A Pair work. **Discuss these questions with a partner.**

1. Do you ever read online message boards? What kinds of things do people discuss there?
2. Why do people like to post on message boards? Do you ever post, or do you just *lurk* (read without answering)?

B Read these posts on a message board and answer the questions.

1. What solution does each writer propose?
2. What reasons do the writers give to support their ideas?

PARENTS.net

Message Board

Today's hot issue: Research has found that 23% of schoolchildren worldwide say they've been bullied at some time. What can schools and communities do about this problem?

Astrid Haugen – *Oslo, Norway*:
There's only one answer to bullying: expel the bullies from school.

Kids need to learn that this behavior is unacceptable. If even minor acts of bullying had serious consequences, parents would keep a closer eye on their children's behavior. Furthermore, kids would be more likely to tell someone that they were being bullied if they knew that there would be a quick solution to their problem.

Many bullies grow up to become violent adults. This kind of behavior must be stopped as soon as it starts.

Eiji Yamada – *Tokyo, Japan*:
I disagree—expelling bullies won't help. Children who bully others have psychological problems, and they need treatment, not punishment.

Instead, we need to educate our children about the harm that bullying causes. Kids must learn to take the problem seriously, and tell a teacher if they see a bullying incident. Also, they must feel a responsibility to help classmates who are being teased and picked on.

All of our children need to feel safe and comfortable at school if they are going to get an education.

Gena Robinson – *Auckland, New Zealand*:
I have one question: Where are the teachers when bullying is taking place? Why aren't they supervising our children?

Without a doubt, class sizes are too large, and teachers are forced to spend too much time on bureaucratic paperwork. Because of this, there are a lot of places in school where no one is watching out for kids—such as lunchrooms, hallways, and playgrounds. It's a known fact that this is where most bullying takes place.

If teachers had time to pay attention to each child, bullying problems would be easier to control.

C Write your own post to this message board on another sheet of paper. State your opinion on what to do about bullying, and give reasons to support your opinion. Add a conclusion.

D Pair work. **Exchange posts with a partner and make suggestions for improvements.**

A Group work. **Get into a group of three people. Choose one of these roles and read about your part as well as the other two.**

Person A: You live in apartment 304 and are married with a nine-month-old baby. Both you and your spouse have to get up at 7:00 A.M. to go to work and take the baby to day care. Your neighbor who lives in apartment 404 makes a lot of noise after midnight—talking and laughing with friends, playing music or watching television. This is keeping you and your family awake—particularly the baby—whose room is just below Person B's living room. The noise has been going on for months, and even though you've left your neighbor notes asking him/her to be quieter, little has changed.

Person B: You live in apartment 404. You work the night shift at a restaurant (which pays more than the day shift), and don't typically get home until after midnight. Though you try to be quiet so that you don't disturb your neighbor in 304, it takes time for you to unwind when you get home from work. You can't go directly to bed. Also, since many places are closed when you finish work, you often have no choice but to go back to your apartment with friends to hang out and talk. Recently, your neighbor in 304 has been leaving you nasty notes. You feel that your neighbor is being unreasonable—especially since he/she is quite noisy in the mornings and argues frequently with his/her spouse—particularly on weekends—when you have time off.

The Building Manager: You manage the apartment building that Persons A and B live in. Person A has come to complain to you about Person B. You've called them together to discuss the problem. Your role is to help the two sides resolve their dispute. Before you meet, make a list of solutions that you could suggest to Person A and Person B.

B Group work. **Follow the directions to do the exercise below. Try to use some of the language for suggesting a compromise.**

The Building Manager
- Begin by asking both sides to state their names and to explain their situations.
- Refer to the list of solutions you created. Suggest these to Person A and Person B. Work with them to reach a compromise that will satisfy both.

Person A and Person B
- Explain your situation to the Building Manager and your neighbor in your own words.
- When the Building Manager offers possible solutions, think about your position, and answer with your opinion. Offer other ideas if appropriate.

Would it be possible to work a different shift at the restaurant?

But if I did that, I wouldn't . . .

Suggesting a compromise

Would it be possible to . . . ?
If he/she were to . . . , would you consider (verb)-ing?
Are you willing to . . . if he/she . . . ?
If he/she should happen to . . . , would you . . . ?

C Group work. **Get together with another group and discuss whether or not you were able to reach a compromise or not. If so, what was it? If not, why not?**

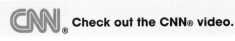 **Check out the CNN® video.** **Practice your English online at elt.thomson.com/worldpass**

Unit 4: Contemporary Issues

A Study the phrases in the box and then use them to complete the sentences below.

> **Word combinations with *peace***
>
> | | | | |
> |---|---|---|---|
> | live in peace | work for peace | a plea for peace | a threat to peace |
> | a peace treaty | the peace process | peace talks | a symbol of peace |

1. At the _____peace talks_____, diplomats are discussing ways to resolve the conflict and end the war.
2. For many people, the white dove is _____a symbol of peace_____
3. After he was elected president, Nelson Mandela worked to help the people of South Africa _____live in peace_____ together.
4. The presidents of the two countries met in Geneva to sign _____a ~~threat to peace~~ peace treaty_____ that ended five years of war.
5. Conflicts over scarce natural resources are _____a threat to peace_____ in many parts of the world.
6. The attack was carried out by a group that is opposed to _____the peace process_____ and is trying to start fighting again.
7. Doctors Without Borders _____work for peace_____ by helping all people injured in a conflict, without taking sides.
8. A group of mothers of soldiers made _____a plea for peace_____ and called for an end to the fighting.

B Review these words from the listening passage "Our cities are growing" on page 41. Then use them to complete the sentences.

> | | | | | |
> |---|---|---|---|---|
> | unchecked | sustainable | forefront | revitalize | slum |
> | proposition | engage in | widespread | advocate (n) | overall |

1. We need to _____revitalize_____ our cities by building new businesses and better housing in the city center.
2. In the _____slum_____ areas of many large cities, people live without electricity, clean water, or safe housing.
3. The capital of my country is experiencing _____~~widespread~~ unchecked_____ growth because thousands of people move there from the countryside every month.
4. UNICEF accepts the _____proposition_____ that all children have a right to good health and a good education.
5. Some people in Brazil _____~~are~~ engage in_____ a process called *participatory democracy* by working together to plan their cities.
6. _____Overall_____, the world's largest cities are continuing to grow rapidly.
7. Many cities suffer from _____widespread_____ poverty and a lack of housing.
8. In many countries, women are in the _____forefront_____ of the environmental movement, and have started many new organizations.
9. The Dalai Lama is a well-known _____advocate_____ for world peace.
10. If something is _____sustainable_____, it can continue for a long time without harming the environment.

> **There's an old saying . . .** *The squeaky wheel gets the grease.*
> If you don't complain about a bad situation, nothing will be done about it. We use this saying to tell someone that they should speak up about a problem.
> "Our boss has made me work every Saturday for the last month. It's not fair!"
> "Well, *the squeaky wheel gets the grease.* You had better say something about it before he writes the schedule for next week."

Expansion Pages

C English has many expressions involving *ears* and *hearing*. Match these expressions and their meanings.

1. turn a deaf ear _c_
2. I'm all ears. _a_
3. I heard it through the grapevine. _g_
4. be up to your ears in something _d_
5. It went in one ear and out the other. _i_
6. have someone's ear _b_
7. grin from ear to ear _e_
8. lend a sympathetic ear _h_
9. I've heard that one before! _f_

a. I'm very interested to hear what you're saying.
b. the person will accept your advice and ideas
c. refuse to listen
d. have far too much of something
e. have a very big smile
f. I don't believe that excuse or explanation.
g. It was a rumor.
h. listen in a kind, friendly way
i. I forgot it as soon as I heard it.

D Use a form of one of the expressions from C to complete these sentences.

1. Don't tell me you left your homework on the train. _I've heard that one before_.
2. I told my boss about the problems with the new computer system, but he _TURNED A DEAF EAR_. He said it worked perfectly.
3. My uncle gave us 20 kg of carrots from his farm. Now we _are up to our ears_ in carrots!
4. I knew you were going to get a promotion. _I heard it through the grapevine_ last week.
5. Whenever I have a problem, I talk to my older sister. She always _lends a sympathetic_ ear.
6. Tell me about your date with Rick! _I'm all ears_.
7. When I saw Debbie, she was _grinning from ear to ear_ because she had just won $5,000 in the lottery.
8. He told me his phone number, but _it went in one ear and out the other_, and now I can't remember it.
9. Professor Park _has the ear_ of many business leaders, and gives them advice about the economy.

In Other Words

A **conflict** is a state of disagreement between people or groups: *The conflict in the Middle East has continued for over 50 years.*

An **argument** is an angry spoken disagreement: *I had a big argument with my parents because they don't want me to buy a car.*

Uninterested means not interested: *I'm completely uninterested in baseball. I think it's boring.*

A **fight** can have a symbolic meaning (as in *fight for women's rights*), but it also means a physical conflict: *Two men were having a fight in the street outside the bar.*

If something is **illegal**, it is against the laws of a place: *In my city, smoking in restaurants is illegal.*

If something is **unethical**, it is morally wrong: *I think it's unethical for teachers to accept presents from their students in exchange for a better grade.*

Unauthorized means without permission from the person or authority: *Jess was reprimanded by the boss for making unauthorized personal phone calls during work time.*

lack

Lack can be a verb:
> *Too many cities lack enough affordable housing.*

It can also be a noun:
> *This lack of housing causes problems for new residents.*

It is NOT an adjective:
> *My city is lack of housing for the growing population.*

UNIT 5

In Other Words

Lesson A | Total immersion

1 VOCABULARY FOCUS

What languages are you studying?

 What are the most difficult factors about learning a foreign language?

Real English
ASL = American Sign Language
(Sign language uses hand
gestures to communicate.)

A Pair work. Read about these people's experiences learning a foreign language. Pay attention to the words and phrases in blue. Then discuss these questions with a partner.

1. What languages is each person studying now and why?
2. How would you describe each person's approximate language level in that language now? Explain your reasons.

Greg Anderson, 19: I'm studying ASL. My professor says that while I may be able to convey basic ideas by signing, I won't be truly proficient for another two or three years. Most of the deaf people I've met have been so patient with my halting ability to sign. This summer I'm going to study at a university for the deaf and hard of hearing. I'll be immersed in deaf culture—and am hoping this will help me to improve skills.

Guy Lagace, 23: I'm French Canadian. My primary language is French and I speak passable English at work. My high school Spanish, however, was pretty rusty, so last summer I spent a month in Guatemala brushing up on the language. At the end of my stay, I could carry on basic conversations. Not bad for only a month of studying.

Akemi Sato, 24: Japanese is my mother tongue. Growing up in Japan, I studied English. At college, I felt that it was important to master at least one other foreign language. On a whim, I decided to study Chinese. Now I am working in China as a Japanese teacher. When I first got here, it was difficult for me to retain words—I was always forgetting new vocabulary.

B Pair work. With a partner, divide the words and phrases in blue from the profiles in A into the following categories:

Adjectives that describe language level or ability: _proficient_____
Verbs that describe using or learning a language: _____
Words that describe one's first language: _____

Real English
whim = sudden,
impulsive desire

C Group work. What is the best way to learn a foreign language? Read the opinions and rank them from 1 (strongly agree) to 5 (strongly disagree). Discuss your answers.

1. ____ Focus exclusively on the new language from the beginning. Don't depend on dictionaries.
2. ____ Immerse yourself in the language and culture. It's the only way to really become proficient.
3. ____ You only need to be able to carry on a basic conversation. Concentrate on learning how to do this.
4. ____ The key to learning any language is to retain what you've studied, so take notes and memorize.
5. ____ To master a foreign language, spend all your time with speakers of that language.

A. Pair work. Acronyms and initialisms are types of abbreviations. Use words from the columns to construct the acronyms and initialisms below. Explain your answers to a partner.

1st word	2nd word	3rd word	4th word
air personal as thank automated to	be soon conditioning teller God identification	announced machine as number it's	Friday possible

1. AC = _air conditioning_____
2. ASAP = _____
3. ATM = _____

4. PIN = _____
5. TBA = _____
6. TGIF = _____

B. Which of the items in **A** might you hear or see:

　a. in an office?　　**b.** at a bank?　　　**c.** in an airport?

2 LISTENING

A TV show about language

A You will hear five short excerpts from a TV series on words and language.
Which episode does each excerpt come from? Listen and check the correct boxes. (CD Tracks 14 & 15)

	1	2	3	4	5
Episode 1: *Language and Personal Identity*	☐	☐	☐	☐	☐
Episode 2: *The History of the English Language*	☐	☐	☐	☐	☐
Episode 3: *Endangered and Dead Languages*	☐	☐	☐	☐	☐

B Listen several times (if necessary) and complete these profiles with the correct information. (CD Track 16)

1. Pilar was born in _____ and grew up speaking _____ at home, but _____ outside her home. Today, she works as a _____ for a _____.
2. The local island language in Guernsey is a dialect of Norman _____. The _____ don't learn the language and usually _____ the island to _____ on the mainland.
3. Many expressions in _____ come from Shakespeare. Many people may be familiar with the expression *one fell swoop*, but they probably don't know the _____ of the word *fell* and what it means.
4. Although Doruk grew up in _____, he now lives in _____, where he doesn't speak the _____ so well. He may have a German _____, but he _____ it's his true identity.
5. _____ is a dead language, but some people are trying to bring it back. Teachers believe that it teaches students _____ skills. They plan to use the _____ to get students interested in studying.

▶ **Ask & Answer**

Should efforts be made to revive languages that are dying out? Why or why not?
How much of your personal identity is connected to the language you speak?

Reduced adverb clauses

A   Read the sentences and underline the adverb clauses. Write *T* for a time clause and *R* for a reason clause.

1. Before he was accepted to college, he studied a lot. __T__
2. He worked part-time while he was attending college. ____
3. Because he was a good student, he won a scholarship to study abroad. ____
4. He became an interpreter after he graduated from college. ____
5. Since he worked in the UN Building, he lived in New York City. ____
6. Because he didn't like New York, he moved to Geneva. ____

> **Adverb clauses**
>
> - Adverb clauses of time and reason tell when or why something happened. They modify the verb or the main clause in a sentence.
> - Many adverb clauses beginning with *before, after, while, because,* and *since* can be reduced and retain the same meaning.

B   Now look at the same sentences. The adverb clauses have been reduced in each case. Notice how the sentences are different from those in **A**.

1. Before he was being accepted to college, he studied a lot.
2. He worked part-time while he was attending college.
3. Because he was Being a good student, he won a scholarship to study abroad.
4. He became an interpreter after he graduated graduating from college.
5. Since he worked Working in the UN Building, he lived in New York City.
6. Because he didn't like Not liking New York, he moved to Geneva.

C   Read these sentences. Underline the subject of each clause and rewrite the sentence if it can be reduced.

1. After their language died out, the villagers tried to revive it.
   can't be reduced

2. Because many expressions in English come from his plays, we should study Shakespeare.
   _____

3. While she spoke Spanish at home, she used English exclusively at work.
   _____

4. Since he moved to Germany two years ago, he's struggled to learn the language.
   _____

5. Before the students took the test, their teacher warned them it would be difficult.
   _____

6. After I mastered Korean, I decided to study Chinese.
   _____

7. Because he studied hard, John passed the test.
   _____

8. Since my mother couldn't speak French, she couldn't communicate with the local people.
   _____

9. Because their parents speak Chinese at home, many second-generation Chinese-Americans grow up speaking the language.
   _____

D   Study the information in the box below.

Reduced adverb clauses with present (-*ing*) and past (-*ed*) participles		
present participle	The car drove into a tree at a high speed, shocking everyone.	This has an active meaning and focuses on the *cause* of the experience.
past participle	**Shocked** by the car accident, Bill called an ambulance.	This has a passive meaning and focuses on the *person* that has the experience.

E Combine these two sentences into one. Start with the word in parentheses.

1. He was frightened by a loud noise. He sat up in bed. (frightened)

   _____

2. He ate dinner. After that, he called his mother. (after)

   _____

3. He juggled two plates. At the same time, he sang a song. (while)

   _____

4. I moved to Spain. I feel calmer. (since)

   _____

5. He pulled out a gun. The bank employees were threatened. (threatening)

   _____

F Read this excerpt from a play called *Late One Night*. Use the correct form of each verb in parentheses. What do you think the note says?

Narrator: It is a cold, windy night. Mary, a young woman, is at home alone, reading a book. We hear a noise upstairs. (1. Frighten) _____ by the noise, Mary walks upstairs to the bedroom door. She opens the door, (2. surprise) _____ the cat.

Mary: Oh, it's only the cat.

Narrator: (3. Embarrass) _____ that she was so scared, Mary smiles to herself. And yet, while (4. relieve) _____, she still looks a little nervous. (5. Comfort) _____ the cat, she returns downstairs. (6. Calm) _____ herself down, she makes a cup of tea. The doorbell rings. When Mary answers the door, there is no one there. (7. Confuse) _____, she looks down to see a small box. (8. Intrigue) _____ by the package, she picks it up and brings it inside.

Mary: I wonder what this is.

Narrator: She opens the box quickly, (9. disappoint) _____ to find it's empty.

Mary: Wait . . . there's a note inside . . .

G Pair work. Now write your own scary scene. You may want to use some of the verbs in the box. Be sure to include a part in your scene for a narrator. Then perform your scene for the class.

alarm	captivate	frighten	puzzle	surprise
bewilder	confuse	relieve	overwhelm	shock

4 SPEAKING

As you can see . . .

A Pair work. **Look at the charts to complete the descriptions. Then label the features of the charts with the words in the box below.**

1. In Spain, in addition to Spanish, _____ other languages are spoken. This pie chart shows that a majority of people speak Spanish, but 17% are speakers of Catalan, and 7% speak _____. The smallest section represents Basque, spoken by _____ of the people.

2. A minority language that nearly disappeared is _____, the language of Wales, in the U.K. But in the last _____ years, more children have been learning Welsh in school and speaking it at home. In this line graph, the horizontal axis represents time, while the vertical axis shows the _____ of Welsh speakers among children 3 to 15 years old.

3. _____ languages are now considered endangered–spoken by only a few elderly people. This bar graph compares the number of endangered languages in different _____. It's clear that _____ is in the biggest danger of losing its linguistic diversity.

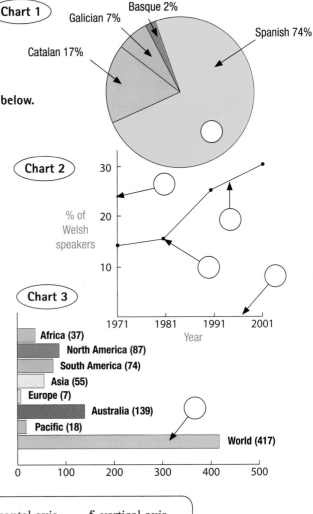

Chart 1 — Spanish 74%, Catalan 17%, Galician 7%, Basque 2%

Chart 2 — % of Welsh speakers — 1971, 1981, 1991, 2001 — Year

Chart 3 — Africa (37), North America (87), South America (74), Asia (55), Europe (7), Australia (139), Pacific (18), World (417) — 0 100 200 300 400 500

| a. line | b. bar | c. section | d. point | e. horizontal axis | f. vertical axis |

B Pair work. **Look at the charts below and discuss these questions with your partner:**

1. What are some important changes that will occur?
2. What effects will these changes have on your country? The world?

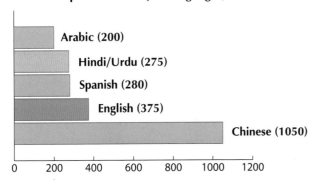

Native Speakers of Major Languages, in millions: 2000 — Arabic (200), Hindi/Urdu (275), Spanish (280), English (375), Chinese (1050) — 0 200 400 600 800 1000 1200

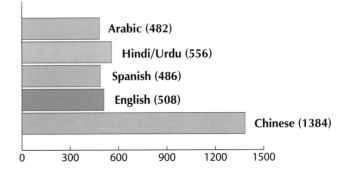

Native Speakers of Major Languages, in millions: 2050 — Arabic (482), Hindi/Urdu (556), Spanish (486), English (508), Chinese (1384) — 0 300 600 900 1200 1500

C Group work. **Look at the different charts on this page. In groups, discuss which information is the most interesting and why. Try to use some of the expressions for talking about charts and data.**

Talking about charts and data	
This chart explains . . .	This ____ represents . . .
As you can see, . . .	This ____ stands for . . .
The key point is that . . .	This ____ shows . . .
It's clear that . . .	This ____ describes . . .
It's important to note that . . .	This ____ compares . . .

UNIT 5

In Other Words

| *Lesson B* | Talk to me. |

1 GET READY TO READ

It's in the writing.

 Do you think men and women have different speaking styles? How about writing styles?

A Pair work. **Read the two e-mail messages. One was written by a man, the other by a woman. Can you tell who wrote which? How? Check your answers on page 168.**

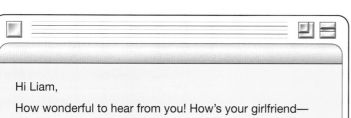

Hi Liam,

How wonderful to hear from you! How's your girlfriend—what was her name—Ciara? I heard that you're planning to visit Spain. Lovely! You'll stay with us, of course. We've got an extra room that overlooks a charming little garden. It's hot here in August, so your best bet is probably to come in September. I'll be on vacation then too, and we can do some sightseeing together.

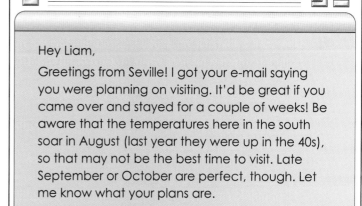

Hey Liam,

Greetings from Seville! I got your e-mail saying you were planning on visiting. It'd be great if you came over and stayed for a couple of weeks! Be aware that the temperatures here in the south soar in August (last year they were up in the 40s), so that may not be the best time to visit. Late September or October are perfect, though. Let me know what your plans are.

B Pair work. **Read the information below, and then discuss these questions.**

1. What did the group of Israeli scientists create?
2. How does the tool work?
3. What belief does the findings of the Israeli scientists' reinforce? Do you agree with this belief? Why or why not?

Professor Moshe Koppel and a group of scientists at Bar Ilan University in Israel have developed a computer program that they say allows them to analyze a piece of writing and to determine with 80% accuracy whether the author is male or female.

Interestingly, the tool does this by analyzing smaller words used in a text (e.g., *the, a, what, and, I, he*). According to Koppel, when one examines this data, certain patterns emerge.

Using the program they developed, Koppel and his team analyzed over 600 texts. What they found was that women's writing included more personal pronouns and possessive adjectives (e.g., *you, he, I, me, her, our,* etc.), while men more often used words such as *a, the, these, that,* as well as numbers, and quantity words such as *a lot.* Koppel has since used this tool to analyze everything from fiction to more "gender-neutral" scientific texts—predicting with 80% accuracy the sex of the writer.

According to some, Professor Koppel's findings only reinforce what many have always believed—that women tend to focus more on people, while men prefer things and ideas.

C Pair work. **Analyze the e-mail messages in A using Professor Koppel's theory. Does it work?**

A Pair work. **Read the statements below and circle** *True* **or** *False.* **Compare your answers with a partner. Then scan the article on page 59 about men's and women's communication styles to find the answers. How many did you get right?**

1. If you talk to a woman about a problem, she's not likely to be a very sympathetic listener. True False
2. For many men, it is important to be in control in a conversation. True False
3. In conversations, women don't give others many chances to speak. True False
4. Women tend to talk more than men in the workplace and classroom. True False

---

Understanding text organization using contrasts

When an author contrasts things, he or she explores differences. Words and phrases such as *but, however, in contrast, on the other hand, though, unlike, whereas,* and *while* are used to signal a contrast.

B **Now read the article on page 59 carefully. How are men's and women's conversational styles different? Complete these sentences with the correct information from the reading.**

1. In conversation, women tend to build rapport and _____. Many men, though, focus on _____.

2. If you tell a woman about a problem, she'll be likely to _____. A man, on the other hand, _____.

3. When women listen to someone, they will often _____. However, men do this less because _____.

4. In public conversations, women will often _____. In contrast, men tend to _____.

5. In personal settings, _____ tend to _____ than _____.

C **Look at the words and phrases in bold in the reading on page 59. Match them with a synonym from the list below.**

1. *thinks* _____
2. *control* _____
3. *talk* _____
4. *indifferent, uncaring* _____
5. *create a connection* _____
6. *result* _____

D Group work. **Do you agree that men's and women's communication styles are generally different? Give examples from your own experience.**

World Link

> **Ask & Answer**
> Do you think the communication styles described in the reading are true for you or the people you know? Why or why not?

One researcher has found that male/female communication differences also apply to e-mail discussion groups. Many more "aggressive" or "sarcastic" remarks are made by male participants, while women tend to contribute many more "supportive" comments.

Source: *Paolo Rossetti* on *iteslj.org*

YOU JUST DON'T GET IT!

For centuries, people have known that men and women communicate differently. Author G.K. Chesterton once said, "Women prefer to talk in twos, while men prefer to talk in threes." More recently, contributions made by linguists and those in the field of gender studies have popularized the notion that *Men are from Mars, Women are from Venus*—not just in terms of how they behave, but how they **converse**. Consider the following example: Ken and Emily, both college students, recently had this
5 conversation:

Ken: How's it goin', Em?
Emily: Not so good. I think that Jane is upset that I was accepted to the study abroad program and she wasn't. She hasn't spoken to me all week or returned my e-mail or phone calls.
K: What? That's silly.
10 **E:** I know. Still . . . it's tough, you know, because we're such good friends.
K: Maybe you ought to talk to a counselor in the program or confront Jane about it.
E: Yeah, well, the thing is that this whole situation makes me feel terrible . . .
K: I know, but I'm serious, Em. Talk to a counselor or Jane sooner rather than later.
E: But, oh . . . never mind, Ken. You just don't get it.
15 **K:** Get what?
E: I *know* that I should talk to Jane and work this thing out.
K: Right, so what's the problem?
E: The *problem* is that I feel bad about it all. I'm just looking for a little understanding . . .
K: I *do* understand, and I think I've suggested something you can do about it.
20 **E:** *(frustrated)* OK, thanks for your advice. Let's change the subject.

> **Real English**
> *Men Are from Mars, Women Are from Venus* = a book by therapist John Gray that explores the differences between men and women

What's going on in the conversation above? According to Deborah Tannen, a professor of linguistics at Georgetown University, men and women often use distinctly different strategies when talking, and the result at times is a total communication breakdown. In conversation, says Tannen, women often work to **build rapport** and make connections. Mention a problem you're having to a woman, for example, and she will likely respond sympathetically first, and then suggest a possible solution. For many
25 men, though, conversation is more akin to what Tannen calls "report-talk" in which the focus is on gathering information and then doing something with it. Mention the same problem to a man, and he will likely give direct feedback or suggest a solution right away.

In Ken and Emily's case, Emily's frustration stems from the fact that she is expecting Ken to listen and offer sympathy, and then perhaps some advice about her situation at school. Ken, on the other hand, hears Emily's story, and in an effort to be helpful,
30 immediately offers a solution to her problem. Emily, though, **perceives** Ken's suggestion as inconsiderate and **dismissive** of her feelings. The result? A breakdown in communication and a mutual sense on both sides that the other just "doesn't get it."

Are you paying attention?

Studies have shown that there are other ways that men's and women's communication styles can lead to misunderstanding. Women, for example, will often use words and phrases like *uh-huh, right, I know what you mean*, or will
35 quickly relate some personal information to show that they're paying attention and are involved in the conversation. However, for men, who typically work to maintain status and control in a conversation, this is often perceived as an attempt to interrupt. Men, therefore, tend to use this strategy less. When a woman is talking and is not receiving this sort of feedback, however, she may think the other person is not listening or isn't interested in what she's saying.

Talk amongst yourselves

40 According to Deborah Tannen, another key element in how men's and women's conversational styles differ is in how much they talk in a given setting. In public settings, such as the workplace and classroom, studies have shown that women ask others for their ideas and give participants frequent opportunities to speak. In contrast, men tend to talk more often and for a longer period of time than women—which results in fewer participants speaking, unless they interrupt. What's the **upshot** of this? A sense, on the part of women, that men tend to **dominate** conversations, and a feeling among men that the women are often a little too quiet
45 or don't have much to say. Interestingly, other studies have shown that in more personal settings, such as on the phone or with friends, women tend to talk more than men. The result? The widespread perception that women, in general, are the more talkative of the two sexes.

What does all this mean?

Is the point of all this to suggest that one conversational style is better than the other? Hardly, say specialists. The key, they
50 say, is to understand that men and women have different ways of communicating. Being aware of these differences will enable us to avoid communication breakdown and to build happier, healthier relationships.

A Read this report and write a heading for each section.

Facilities for Neptunian Speakers in Metroville

Introduction

This report describes and assesses the facilities available for Neptunians in our city. In the past ten years, the number of Neptunian speakers has increased considerably, due to the large number of extraterrestrial companies that have established branch offices here.

1. _____

Metroville offers a number of news and entertainment sources for Neptunian speakers. TV3 has a Neptunian-language news broadcast daily at 11:30 P.M., and several radio stations have daily Neptunian programming. Neptunian newspapers are available, but they are generally several days old. On the whole, Neptunian speakers report that the Internet is their main source of news. Neptunian movies with subtitles are frequently shown at downtown movie theaters, and videos and DVDs dubbed in Neptunian can be rented at many stores.

2. _____

Metroville has two Neptunian-medium schools. In general, extraterrestrial children ages 5–14 attend Metroville Intergalactic School, where all classes are taught in Neptunian. There is also a smaller school, Intergalactic Academy, for children ages 6–12. At present, there is no Neptunian high school in this region of the country, so high school students must attend boarding schools in other cities.

3. _____

Very few of the emergency services telephone operators understand Neptunian. Last year, an extraterrestrial patient died in a waiting room at Metroville Hospital because he was unable to communicate his problem to the nurses there. Many doctors and nurses speak Neptunian, but they are not always available to translate.

4. _____

Metroville provides good educational and entertainment facilities for its Neptunian-speaking residents, but emergency services remain a problem. It is recommended that the government set up a special emergency telephone number for extraterrestrials, with Neptunian-speaking operators. In addition, it would be advisable to provide extraterrestrial residents with a list of doctors who speak Neptunian. Finally, the government should consider supporting an intergalactic high school.

B Find, underline, and label these things in the report in **A**.

a. an expression introducing the purpose of the report
b. two expressions for talking about overall patterns
c. two expressions for making recommendations

C You are a member of the National Committee for Better Education, and you have been asked to provide information on the status of foreign languages in your country. Write a report with four short sections and give a heading to each one. Report the following:

> ### Writing a report
>
> A report is an objective summary of facts on a topic, written in an impersonal style. It is usually divided into sections with separate headings, and may contain a series of recommendations at the end.

1. the importance of foreign languages in your country
2. the current situation of foreign language teaching in schools
3. opportunities for learning foreign languages outside of the school system
4. recommendations for improving people's foreign language ability in your country

D Pair work. Exchange reports with your partner and make suggestions for improving each other's report.

4 COMMUNICATION

Debate the issue

A Group work. **Get into groups of four. Read this statement and then take one of the roles below.**

> Everyone in the world should have to learn a second language.

Student A: You are IN FAVOR OF the statement above.	Student B: You are AGAINST the statement above.	Students C & D: You are the JUDGES.
• On a piece of paper, make a list of as many reasons as you can that will support your side of the argument. • Try to anticipate some of the points your opponent will make. • Study the rules for debate below.		Listen to the two sides debate the topic. Your role is not to agree with one side or another, but to moderate the debate and to ultimately decide which side argued better—based on the rules for debate below. Take notes as you listen to the two sides.

Rules for debate
• State each reason in your argument clearly.
• Use facts or other data to support your point.
• Do not go over the time limit (see B).
• Important: Don't introduce ideas randomly. When you offer a rebuttal, make sure that it's related to something your opponent has just said.
• At the end of the debate, summarize your arguments briefly.

B Group work. **Get together with your group and begin the debate.**

1. Student A begins by stating his or her first point. Time limit: 45 seconds
2. Student B responds with an opposing idea. Time limit: 45 seconds
3. Repeat steps one and two for 3–4 rounds.
4. Then each side should summarize its main points.
5. The Judges will compare notes, choose a winner, and explain their decision.

> *I think everyone should have to learn a second language because . . .*

> *Yes, but on the other hand . . .*

C Group work. **Choose one of the statements below. Then switch roles and repeat the exercises in A and B.**

• Second-language learning should begin when children are in the first grade.
• A language teacher should be a native speaker of that language.
• A government should protect endangered languages in its country.

 Check out the CNN® video. **Practice your English online at** elt.thomson.com/worldpass

Unit 5: In Other Words

A Study the phrases in the box and use them to complete the sentences below.

> **Word combinations with *discussion***
>
> take part in a discussion   under discussion
> broaden the discussion   a pointless discussion
> generate a discussion   a great deal of discussion
> a heated discussion

1. This is _____! We're arguing about where to go out for dinner, but we don't have any money!
2. We need to _____ about immigration and hear more different points of view.
3. In the kitchen, two chefs were having _____ about how to cook the sauce, and all the customers in the restaurant could hear them shouting.
4. Our teacher likes to ask us questions about the news in order to _____.
5. A plan to build a swimming pool in Memorial Park is _____ by the city council.
6. I want to _____ about energy conservation at the environmental conference next week.
7. At the employee meeting, there was _____ about the new vacation schedule. We talked for two hours.

B Circle the word or expression in each line that doesn't belong.

1. native language	mother tongue	first language	sign language
2. difficult	proficient	skillful	fluent
3. retain	lose	remember	acquire
4. expression	idiom	phrase	verb
5. passable	halting	rusty	poor
6. conversation	dialog	speech	discussion

> **I didn't know that!**
> The words *grammar* and *glamour* originally came from the same root, the Greek word for *letter*. In the Middle Ages, *grammar* came to mean all forms of knowledge. People at that time thought that science was a mysterious form of magic. In Scotland, *grammar* was pronounced *glamour*, and *glamour* became a term for magic spells. Nowadays, *glamour* means a mysterious attractiveness—but most students don't see any *glamour* in *grammar*!

C Where is it spoken? Match the language with a country where it is spoken, using your dictionary as needed.

1. Swahili ___   a. Brazil
2. Farsi ___   b. Philippines
3. Urdu ___   c. Iran
4. Arabic ___   d. Egypt
5. Filipino ___   e. India
6. Portuguese ___   f. Pakistan
7. French ___   g. Kenya
8. Hindi ___   h. Canada

Expansion Pages

D Review these words and phrases from the reading "You just don't get it!" on page 59.
Then use them in the correct form to complete the sentences.

> build rapport   feedback   perceive   dismissive   dominate   widespread   upshot   interrupt

1. I hate it when my boyfriend _____ me while I'm speaking. I never get to finish what I'm saying!
2. Whenever I have dinner with my parents, my mother _____ the conversation with news about all of my old friends who have already gotten married.
3. After I gave my presentation, I got good _____ from my colleagues. They said I explained everything very clearly.
4. There is a _____ belief that women talk more than men, but research shows that that isn't true.
5. The _____ of Dr. Tannen's book is that we need to understand that men and women have different ways of communicating.
6. My boss is always so _____ of my ideas. She doesn't listen, and she doesn't take them seriously.
7. Women sometimes _____ men as being inconsiderate because they give advice instead of just listening.
8. An important part of conversation is to _____ with other people.

E Spell check! These words were taken from a list of those most commonly misspelled by native speakers of English. Rewrite them correctly. Three of them have no mistakes—write OK by them.

1. allready   _____
2. ilegal   _____
3. address   _____
4. develope   _____
5. ocurred   _____
6. February   _____
7. proffessor   _____
8. saftey   _____
9. recieve   _____
10. afect   _____
11. def inate   _____
12. twelvth   _____
13. suceed   _____
14. goverment   _____
15. disapear   _____
16. jewelery   _____
17. assistent   _____
18. unbeliveable   _____
19. forty   _____
20. neccessary   _____

> ### In Other Words
>
> A **language** is a system of spoken and (usually) written communication that is used by the people of a particular country or region: *Chinese is the world's most widely spoken language.*
> A **dialect** is a variety of a language spoken in a particular area: *People used to be surprised when I first moved to Tokyo because I spoke the Osaka dialect of Japanese.*
> An **accent** is the way you pronounce words when you speak: *When I heard the woman's accent, I could tell that she came from the southern part of our country.*
>
> **Slang** means informal language used by a particular group of people, such as teenagers: *Americans have a lot of slang words for money, such as* dough *and* bucks.
> **Jargon** is words used by experts in a subject, which other people don't understand: *I tried to read the manual for my laptop, but it was all written in computer jargon.*
> **Terminology** is vocabulary that's used only in a particular field: *I had a broken leg, or a fractured tibia in medical terminology.*

> slang
> *Slang* is a noncount noun. Therefore, it cannot be used in the plural.
> *My friend is teaching me American slang.*
> *I've learned a lot of good slangs.*
> *I've learned a lot of good slang expressions.*

Ordinary People, Extraordinary Lives

| Lesson A | Follow your dream! |

1 VOCABULARY FOCUS

A well-kept secret

WARM UP

Look at the photos and read the title of the article below. What do you think the article is going to be about?

A Pair work. **Read this article about Peter Alvarez. Then close your books and take turns telling your partner his story.**

Changing Gears

(1) "I've always loved to cook," says newscaster Peter Alvarez with a twinkle in his eye. "I remember having aspirations to grow up and become a chef. Somewhere along the way, I got sidetracked, and I fell into broadcasting."

And it's been quite a storied career for Mr. Alvarez. The only child of working-class parents, he started at the bottom and worked his way to the top to become one of the most watched TV reporters on the evening news.

(2) Cooking came back into his life in an unexpected way. He bumped into an old high school friend of his on a flight to Mexico City. As it turned out, his friend was attending cooking classes and invited Peter to join her.

From that first class, Peter was hooked. Soon he was juggling his busy day job at the TV station along

with his full-time studies in pastry cooking at night. "I was channeling all my energy into the cooking and neglecting my regular job. And I was getting exhausted—it's not easy to wear three hats . . . as broadcaster, pastry student, and parent."

After a year of studies, Peter realized that he wanted to study with some of the more renowned pastry chefs in France. With his family's blessing, he took some time off and flew to France.

(3) Upon his return, he knew what he had to do—quit the TV station. His resignation initially caused quite a stir, since he had been such a fixture at Channel 4. When asked what his plans were, he smiled and said, "Don't worry. I have something in mind . . ."

That "something" was working as an apprentice to the pastry chef at the acclaimed Barbar Hotel. How does he feel about swapping his role as glamorous TV personality for that of kitchen assistant?

"I couldn't be happier," he beams. And we couldn't be happier for him, either.

B Pair work. Look back at the article in A and with a partner find the words and expressions that have the same meaning.

Section 1	1. distracted; diverted _____ 2. having an interesting history _____ 3. dreams; goals _____	4. a bright sparkle _____ 5. unexpectedly ended up doing _____
Section 2	1. famous, well-respected _____ 2. focusing; directing _____ 3. approval _____	4. met unexpectedly _____ 5. doing several things at the same time _____
Section 3	1. thinking about an idea _____ 2. surprised; shocked _____ 3. exchanging _____	4. permanent feature _____ 5. assistant _____

C Group work. Discuss these questions.

1. What aspirations did you have as a child?
2. Why do you think people get sidetracked in their lives?
3. What is something in the news that has caused a stir recently? What exactly happened?
4. If you had all the free time you wanted, what would you channel your energy into?
5. Complete this sentence: *If I could, I would swap my _____ for _____.*

>>> Vocabulary Builder ▲ ....

Read these sentences and match each underlined expression with its definition in the box.

> **a.** already known and not interesting   **c.** admire   **e.** immediately
> **b.** perform more than one job or task   **d.** not tell anyone

1. I have to take my hat off to her. She finished the project under budget. _____
2. He was secretly studying at the pastry school and had to keep it under his hat. _____
3. That gossip about Britney Spears is old hat. I heard it last month. _____
4. I wear two hats: during the day I'm a teacher and at night I'm a singer in a rock band. _____
5. Don't encourage him. He'll start telling terrible jokes at the drop of a hat. _____

2 LISTENING
Running ultramarathons

A Pair work. You are going to hear an interview with Duncan, a man who competes in very long races called "ultramarathons." Look at the chart below. Can you predict any of the answers you will hear? Write your predictions on a separate piece of paper.

Average marathon distance	_____ miles _____ yards OR _____ kilometers
Possible ultramarathon distance	_____ miles OR _____ kilometers
Examples of ultramarathon timed races	_____ hours AND _____ hours
Temperature during desert race	_____ Fahrenheit OR _____ Celsius

 B Now listen to the first part of the interview and complete the chart in A. (CD Track 17)

C Now listen to the entire interview and circle *T* for true or *F* for false.
Write key words to support your answers. (CD Track 18)

1. Duncan depends on luck to some degree.	T	F	_____
2. He doesn't like the feeling when he's running.	T	F	_____
3. He's eaten pizza during a race.	T	F	_____
4. He always takes breaks to sleep.	T	F	_____
5. He started running because he was ambitious.	T	F	_____
6. He says you need five years' running experience.	T	F	_____

▶ **Ask & *Answer***

What do you think of Duncan's passion for running? What are some of the healthy and unhealthy aspects of being enthusiastic about something?

3 LANGUAGE FOCUS

Reported speech

A **Study the information in the box.**

We use reported speech to "report" to another person what someone else has said.
  Quoted speech: "I have something in mind," he said.
  Reported speech: He said (that) he had something in mind.
We use reporting verbs to introduce the reported statement.
  They reported (that) she had left her job.
  My mother told me not to go.
The verb in the reported statement may shift in reported speech.
  Quoted speech: "I've been to Europe three times," he said.
  Reported speech: He said (that) he had been to Europe three times.

Say and *tell*

He said (to me) (that) he had run two marathons.

Other verbs like *say: announce, complain, mention, propose, reply, report*

He told me (that) he had run two marathons.
He told me to train hard for the race.

Other verbs like *tell: advise, ask, convince, instruct, persuade, remind*

B Pair work. **With a partner, read these sentences and choose the appropriate reporting verb.
Then underline the changes from quoted speech to reported speech.**

1. "Your papers are due on Friday."
   The teacher ___b___ us that our papers were due on Friday.
   a. proposed   **b.** told   **c.** announced

2. "She's guilty."
   I didn't agree, but finally he _____ me that she was guilty.
   a. convinced   **b.** admitted   **c.** proposed

3. "The meeting has definitely been canceled."
   They _____ (that) the meeting had definitely been canceled.
   a. announced   **b.** advised   **c.** told

4. "Don't forget. It's getting late and you need to get up early tomorrow."
   He _____ me it was getting late and that I needed to get up early the next day.
   a. said   **b.** reminded   **c.** mentioned

5. "Mary, you should take some time off and enjoy yourself."
   He _____ (that) she should take some time off and enjoy herself.
   a. persuaded   **b.** proposed   **c.** instructed

6. "My shoes are hurting my feet."
   She _____ (that) her shoes were hurting her feet.
   a. advised   **b.** told   **c.** complained

66 Unit 6 • Ordinary People, Extraordinary Lives

C Look at the information in the chart. What follows the reporting verb in *yes/no* and *wh-* questions? What do you notice about the word order?

Reported questions
"Where do you live?" he asked. → He asked where I lived.
"Are you happy?" she asked. → She asked if I was happy (or not).
She asked whether (or not) I was happy.
She asked whether I was happy (or not).

D A female news reporter is interviewing a man who runs ultramarathons. Read part of the interview below. Then rewrite each sentence in reported speech.

1. Q: How many marathons have you run?
2. A: I completed my fourth one yesterday.
3. Q: Who do you train with?
4. A: I train with my brother.

5. Q: Do you have a family?
6. A: Yes, I do.
7. Q: Do they approve of your running?
8. A: They don't love it, but they accept it.

1. _____
2. _____
3. _____
4. _____

5. _____
6. _____
7. _____
8. _____

E Read this letter Pat wrote about her new friend. Find the seven errors in reported speech and correct them.

Dear Mom and Dad,

Campus life has been great so far. I'm studying hard and making new friends. One of my new friends sits next to me in history class. Her name is Ethel. She says that she was 70 years old! I don't believe her.

I asked Ethel why she did wait so long to go back to college. She told to me that she had had to raise a family and work, so she couldn't go to college. I asked her where was she working before she became a student. She said that she was retired to me.

I also asked her if or not she liked college life. She said she loved it! I really admire Ethel because she's so upbeat. I asked her what your secret was. She told me that she always looks at the bright side of things.

Anyway, I'll write again soon.

Love, Pat

F Pair work. Imagine that you are a reporter. You are going to interview your partner for a special interest story. Ask your partner these questions and add three questions of your own.

1. What have you done in your life that is different?
2. What made you decide to do it?
3. Is there anything you wish you hadn't done?

4. _____
5. _____
6. _____

G Pair work. Now tell another partner about your interview. Describe the questions you asked and the responses you received.

> I asked Anita what she had done in her life that was different. She replied that she had . . .

A Group work. **Discuss these questions.**

1. Have you ever spoken to a group in your native language? In English?
2. What are some situations in which people have to make presentations?
3. How do you feel about speaking in front of a group? Why do you feel that way?

B Group work. **Read this student's presentation. How is a presentation similar to an essay? How is it different?**

> Today, I'd like to tell you about a person who has had a very big influence on my life—my Aunt Rita. Her husband died when I was very young, and she came to live with my family. She was like a second mother to me and my brothers.
>
> One thing Aunt Rita did was to teach me to love books and reading. Every year, on my birthday, she took me to a bookstore and let me choose any book I wanted. She read stories to me every night when I was little, and helped me learn to read when I started school. She also taught me to love nature. My parents both worked very long hours, so Aunt Rita always took us to the zoo or the park, and helped us plant a flower garden. But most importantly, Aunt Rita encouraged my dreams, even when they seemed hopeless. After high school, I wanted to go overseas and study environmental science. I knew my family couldn't afford that, but Aunt Rita persuaded me to apply for a scholarship, and I was able to come here to this university.
>
> In conclusion, my Aunt Rita has had a very important influence on my life, and my future. If she hadn't encouraged me, I wouldn't be a student here today. Thank you.

C You are going to give a short presentation (about two minutes) about a person who has had an important influence on you, such as a teacher or family member. Plan your presentation by completing the outline with words and short phrases.

A person who has influenced me

Person's name: _____

Words or phrases describing the person: _____, _____, _____

Ways this person has influenced me:

    1. _____

    Example: _____

    2. _____

    Example: _____

    3. _____

    Example: _____

Conclusion: How would your life be different without this person? _____

D Pair work. **Practice giving your presentation to a partner. Your partner will time you and give you advice for improving your presentation.**

E Group work. **Work with a group of four. Take turns giving your presentations. While you listen to each speaker, make notes about these things on a slip of paper. When all the speakers have finished, give them your notes.**

> voice:
>
> eye contact:
>
> best thing about the presentation:

Presentation phrases
Introducing a presentation
Today, I'm going to talk to you about . . .
I'd like to tell you about . . .
In this presentation, I'm going to . . .
Ending a presentation
Before I finish, let me say . . .
So in conclusion, . . .
To conclude, . . .

UNIT 6
Ordinary People, Extraordinary Lives

Lesson B | The kindness of strangers

1 GET READY TO READ

A helping hand

WARM UP

Have you ever been in a situation in which you had to ask someone you didn't know for help? What happened?

A Pair work. **Look at the photos below and describe to your partner the people and what is happening in each one.**

2.

3.

Guessing meaning from context

To guess the meaning of important but unfamiliar words in a text:
- Think about how the word is related to the overall topic.
- Read the surrounding sentences. These often include information that will give clues to the meaning of the new word.
- Notice prefixes, suffixes, and familiar parts of the word, e.g., *displeased* = *dis-* + *pleased*.

B Pair work. **Study the box in A. Then look at the underlined words in each sentence below and discuss these questions with a partner.**

- Without looking at a dictionary, what do you think each underlined word means?
- What information helped you to understand the meaning of the underlined words?

1. How did I get here? I used to have a job, an apartment, nice clothes. Now look at me. I'm <u>filthy</u> from not bathing for days. My clothes are torn and stained with food. Who'll help me now?

2. We got off the train at the wrong stop and had no idea where we were. We were completely <u>disoriented</u>. There were no other trains for the rest of the day, and we were worried we'd be <u>stranded</u> in that strange place overnight.

3. The drought has hit this part of the country very hard and water is scarce. People are forced to survive on a <u>meager</u> diet of rice and milk. As a result, many—especially young children—are suffering from <u>malnutrition</u>. As relief organizations work out the logistics of bringing in clean water and giving out food, people grow more desperate and tensions in the region are rising.

> **Ask & Answer**
> Think about the situations above. If you encountered people like this on the street or saw an ad asking for help, what would you do?

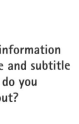

HAÏTI

Gonaïves

Port-au-Prince ★

- Located in the Caribbean
- **Capital city:** Port-au-Prince
- **Official languages:** Creole, French
- One of the poorest countries in the world
- In 2004 was struck by a powerful hurricane that left thousands dead or homeless

A Pair work. **Read this background information about Haiti. Then look at the title and subtitle of the reading on page 71. What do you think the story is going to be about?**

B Read the entire article. As you read, use the strategy you practiced in Get Ready to Read on page 69 to understand the meaning of unfamiliar words and phrases.

C Pair work. **Look at the underlined words and phrases in the reading. Which category do they belong in? Complete the chart and then compare answers. Discuss the meaning of the expressions with a partner.**

describing positioning or a lack of space	under water	describing things moving quickly	describing something very messy or smelling bad	describing something blocked
sandwiched between				

D Read the article on page 71 again and complete the sentences by circling the correct answer. Then find key words in the reading that support your answers and write them on the line below.

1. The conditions on the tap-tap were very comfortable / crowded.

   _____

2. Recently, life in Haiti has been calm / chaotic.

   _____

3. The city of Gonaïves was hit hard / escaped major damage when Hurricane Jeanne struck.

   _____

4. The young man from Gonaïves was very anxious / relieved as he talked about his situation.

   _____

5. The young man from Gonaïves was poorly / well dressed.

   _____

6. The passengers had / didn't have a lot, but they were stingy / generous.

   _____

E Pair work. **Using the key words in the chart, take turns with a partner to retell the story in your own words.**

Student A	Student B
tap-tap	filthy clothes
Port-au-Prince	white polo shirt
hurricane	market lady
young man from Gonaïves	ten-gourde note

▶ **Ask & *Answer***

Why do you think the author wrote this story? What do you think his message is? Has someone ever helped you in a time of need? Explain what happened.

ON THE TAP-TAP After the storm, a generous spirit shines through in Haiti

by Kent Annan, from Orion

"Leve pye ou." Lift your feet. "Fon ti avanse." Move over a bit. I was sandwiched between two middle-aged ladies up near the front of a freight truck converted for passengers, a large version of the public-transportation vehicles that Haitians call "tap-taps." Women who had been selling goods all day at the market stuffed their sacks and baskets under benches that ran along the sides. The middle aisle filled with cargo, people crammed into the center. Others hung out the back door.
5 Almost everything in Haiti seemed scarce; seats to Port-au-Prince in the late afternoon were no exception.

The tap-tap jostled to a start after a driver's assistant banged loudly on the metal siding. Talk soon turned to Gonaïves. Forty miles in the opposite direction, Haiti's fourth-largest city was submerged after Hurricane Jeanne hit it a week earlier. People were still stranded on rooftops. Aid was slow to arrive; relief organizations could not deal with the logistics, armed gangs, and mobs of desperate people.

10 It was late September, 2004. In less than a year, this small island country of eight million people had experienced political upheaval, flooding that killed three thousand, malnourishment, widespread unemployment, and, now, hurricane flooding that had killed two thousand more. From a distance, those watching the news must wonder how anybody makes it in Haiti. Living here, I sometimes wonder too, but less so because I see the little things.

After passengers expressed how terrible the situation was in Gonaïves, a young man, about 20 years old, spoke up. "I'm
15 from Gonaïves," he said. "Just got out." Conversation in the front half of the tap-tap quieted. He told of bodies, of water sweeping the living away to join the dead, of mad stampedes threatening any meager supplies of potable water or food. His Creole was rapid-fire and he seemed a little disoriented as he jumped between subjects. His eyes darted to different people as he talked.

People asked questions. Bridges were down, roads nearly impassable. Did he slog through the mud and water? Yes. He
20 left to find help, leaving his mother and siblings behind. Would he return soon? Yes, he hoped.

"There's nothing, nothing," he kept saying. "These clothes. Look. I've been wearing them since last Saturday." Haitians are almost always immaculately groomed, but the young man from Gonaïves was filthy. Little bits of straw and other debris littered his hair. His shirt and baggy jean shorts were stained and ragged.

Suddenly a middle-aged man reached into a plastic bag and gave him a white polo shirt. "Here. Take this," he said.
25 "Thank you," said the young man. The crowd immediately told him to take off his old shirt and put on the new one. When he did, a sharp, rancid smell was released. Within 30 seconds, someone gave him a white T-shirt. A pair of green shorts appeared. A comb. Someone else gave him a bar of soap.

Meanwhile, one of the market ladies had taken a crumpled 10-gourde note (about 28 cents) out of the fold of her skirt and squeezed her way through the tap-tap from person to person, saying, "Just give what you can. Five gourdes, ten gourdes,
30 fifty gourdes, anything." After completing her circuit, she handed the young man a fistful of bills and coins.

He was holding on to the roof rail with his right hand, revealing a few small holes in the armpit of his new shirt. He looked around. Then he started wiping tears from his eyes. "Mwen pa konnen . . ." I don't know . . ."You didn't even ask for anything, we just want to give. We're all Gonaïveians now," people said, and then were quiet for a little while as the tap-tap bounded on toward Port-au-Prince.

Source: *Orion,* Jan/Feb 2005
187 Main St. Great Barrington, MA 01230
www.oriononline.org

Real English
make it = survive
get out in time = escape just before something bad happens
sibling = brother or sister

A Read this biography and answer the questions that follow.

Jane Goodall is one of the world's most important researchers on animal behavior, and a strong environmental advocate. She has given her whole life to the conservation of the rainforest and animal species.

Goodall was born in London in 1934. She loved animals when she was a child, and dreamed of working in Africa. In 1956, she was invited to visit a friend's family in Kenya. There she met Dr. Louis Leakey, a famous anthropologist who was looking for someone to carry out research on chimpanzees. Jane got the job, and in 1960, she arrived in Tanzania. For more than 20 years, she lived with the chimpanzees and made many important scientific discoveries about their behavior.

But in the 1980s, Goodall became very concerned about the disappearance of the rainforest. She left Tanzania and founded the Jane Goodall Institute, which has programs to help the people of the rainforest and preserve the environment for rainforest animals. She now travels more than 300 days every year, giving presentations about the importance of conservation. She has also founded *Roots and Shoots*, an international network of 7,000 youth groups.

Jane Goodall's work with chimpanzees has inspired people around the world, and her youth groups are taking action on local problems worldwide. Her efforts have made the world better for both animals and people.

1. What order is used in presenting the information?
2. What is in the introduction?
3. What is in the conclusion?

B Read this information about Nelson Mandela and write a biography. You do NOT need to use all of the facts.

Nelson Mandela

marriages:	(1) Evelyn Ntoko (1944) (2) Winnie Madikizela (1958) (3) Graca Machel (1998)
autobiography:	*Long Walk to Freedom*, 1994
Nobel Peace Prize:	1993
favorite time of day:	sunset
after retirement:	raised money for children's charities
first language:	Xhosa
first job:	herding family's cattle (age 5)
education:	mission school; Union College of Fort Hare; studied law in Johannesburg
family:	parents Gadla and Nodekeni, 3 sisters
prison:	sentenced to life term for anti-government activities; released after 27 years, February 11, 1990
joined African National Congress (ANC):	1942
positions in ANC:	1947: Youth League Secretary; 1952: Deputy Head of ANC; 1991: President of ANC
goal of ANC:	to end the unjust system of apartheid in South Africa
ANC outlawed:	1960
favorite music:	classical (Handel, Tchaikovsky)
born:	Qunu, South Africa, July 18, 1918
first democratically elected president of South Africa:	1994–1999 (62% of vote)

World Link

The greatest glory in living lies not in never falling, but in rising every time we fall. – Nelson Mandela

C Pair work. Exchange papers with a partner and discuss the similarities and differences in your biographies.

4 COMMUNICATION

Person of the Year

A Pair work. **Read the description of Person of the Year, and then about some people who have won the award. What do you think of these choices? Discuss with a partner.**

Person of the Year—At the end of every year, the U.S. magazine *Time* features an issue dedicated to The Person of the Year. The award is given to individuals as well as couples, groups of people, machines, or places. The Person of the Year is chosen for the influence (positive or negative) that this person or thing has had on society and the world over the course of the year. Some of *Time's* selections have included:

Year	Person	Reason
1927	Charles Lindbergh	the first person to win the award; chosen for making the first solo transatlantic flight from North America to Paris
1938	Adolf Hitler	head of Germany's Nazi party who triggered World War II
1966	The Generation of People 25 and Under	selected for their influence on politics, pop culture, and society
1982	The Personal Computer	selected as low-cost PCs begin making their appearance in more businesses, universities, and some homes
1996	Dr. David Ho	doctor selected for the work he's done in AIDS research
1999	Jeff Bezos	founder of amazon.com chosen for his role in influencing how we shop and do business

B **Read the directions and fill in your choice and reason.**

You are an editor who works for a popular online magazine that readers around the world subscribe to. This year, your magazine is publishing an issue that is dedicated to The Person of the Year. The criteria you use to make your selection are as follows:

- The Person of the Year can be an individual, a couple, a group, an organization or company, or a generation of people. It can also be an object or invention—for example, some kind of video game that has had a profound influence on people.

- Your nomination should take into account how profound an influence the person, group, or object has had on society and the world in the last year. This influence can be positive *or* negative.

The Person of the Year: _____

Reason(s): _____

C Group work. **Get into a group of three to four people and compare and discuss your choices. As a team, choose *one* Person of the Year to nominate. Write your nomination on the board.**

D Class work. **Look at the list of nominations on the board. Take a class vote to determine who The Person of the Year for your class will be.**

 Check out the CNN® video. **Practice your English online at elt.thomson.com/worldpass**

Expansion Pages

A Study the phrases in the box and match them with their meanings.

Word combinations with *life*	
1. lose your life ___	a. a complete change in your life
2. risk your life ___	b. put yourself in great danger
3. save your life ___	c. How are you? *(informal)*
4. a matter of life and death ___	d. die
5. your social life ___	e. Don't waste your time worrying! *(informal)*
6. a new life ___	f. keep you from dying
7. Life's too short! ___	g. an extremely serious situation
8. How's life? ___	h. your friendly relationships

B Complete the sentences with one of the phrases from A, making all necessary changes.

1. Hi, Russ. _____ I haven't seen you in ages!
2. Sachi is moving to Los Angeles because she wants to forget all her problems and start

   _____
3. Knowing how to swim is important because it can _____ in an emergency.
4. Firefighters _____ every day when they run into burning buildings to rescue people.
5. For children in poor countries, access to clean water is _____. Many of them die every year from diseases carried by water.
6. You should stop thinking about your old boyfriend all the time. _____
7. Over 200 people _____ in the hurricane last month, and thousands more were injured.
8. I was very lonely when I first moved to this city, but then I started meeting people and

   _____ improved.

> **There's an old saying . . .** *Actions speak louder than words.*
>
> What a person actually does is more important than what he or she says. We use this saying to tell people that they need to do what they say they will do.
>
> "I'm really sorry for making such a mess in the kitchen, Mother."
> "Well, *actions speak louder than words.* How about doing the dishes?"

C Study the underlined words. Then match the sentence parts.

1. She admitted ___	a. to talk to a lawyer.
2. She complained ___	b. that the meeting would be held at 2:00.
3. She reminded us ___	c. to bring our dictionaries to class tomorrow.
4. She advised us ___	d. that we should have a party on the last day of class.
5. She mentioned ___	e. that she had stolen $50,000 from her employer.
6. She announced ___	f. that she'd seen him, but she didn't say where.
7. She proposed ___	g. that her children never called her on her birthday.

D Skim the reading "On the Tap-Tap" on page 71 and review these words.
Then use them to complete the sentences below.

disoriented	immaculately	submerged	filthy
impassable	scarce	strandedupheaval	

1. I missed the last bus, and I couldn't afford a taxi, so I was _____ in the city late at night.
2. After the earthquake, the roads were _____ because of the damage.
3. My grandmother keeps her kitchen _____ clean. I don't know how she does it!
4. The accident victims seemed _____ when they climbed out of the wrecked bus.
5. In the desert, water is very _____.
6. The boat hit a rock that was _____ under the water, and two hours later it sank.
7. The little boys were _____ after playing soccer in the mud all afternoon.
8. The change in government caused a major _____ in the country.

E Read these sentences describing people's character and write the adjective that means the same thing after them.
Use your dictionary as needed.

intelligent	dishonest	annoying	generous	unfriendly	strange

1. My neighbor has a heart of gold. _____
2. His brother is a real cold fish. _____
3. Our new colleague is kind of an oddball. _____
4. Your sister is really a quick study. _____
5. Her new boyfriend is sort of a shady character. _____
6. My boss can be a real pain in the neck! _____

In Other Words

Extraordinary has a positive meaning when applied to a person: *My grandfather was an extraordinary man who taught high school for 50 years.*
Exceptional means someone or something is unusually good: *Tiger Woods is an exceptional golfer who began playing at the age of three.*
Unusual is neutral: *My youngest sister has a very unusual name.*
Strange and **odd** are both slightly negative: *A strange old woman lives in the house next door. She never talks to anybody. / He asked me an odd question.*

If someone is **famous**, they are known in many places: *Oprah Winfrey is a famous TV personality.*
If someone is **eminent**, they are respected by other people in their field: *Dr. Kim is an eminent heart surgeon who developed new life-saving techniques.*
If someone is **renowned**, they are admired by many people: *Mother Theresa was renowned for her work with the poor.*
Notorious means famous for doing something bad: *D.B. Cooper was a notorious plane hijacker in the U.S.*

Watch out!

excellent
Excellent is an absolute term, and so does not have a comparative or superlative form:
Michael Jordan was the most excellent basketball player in history.
Michael Jordan was the most successful basketball player in history.

Review: Units 4–6

1 LANGUAGE CHECK

On a separate sheet of paper, rewrite the sentences using the words
or grammatical indications in parentheses and making all necessary changes.

1. It rained on Saturday, so we couldn't go to the beach. (if)
2. Because they didn't want to wake up the baby, they spoke quietly. (*reduced clause*)
3. "Are you interested in studying abroad next year?" (My teacher asked)
4. We have a lot of homework, so we can't go to the movie with you. (if)
5. "Quit smoking and lose ten kilos!" (My doctor)
6. "I had been working for an hour when my computer crashed." (Lia said)
7. I didn't set my alarm clock, so I was late for class. (if)
8. "Four languages are spoken in Spain." (Jorge told us)
9. Before he became a successful actor, Jared worked as a waiter. (*reduced clause*)
10. He got in a bad car accident while he was driving on a mountain road. (*reduced clause*)
11. "Susan, how many marathons have you run?" (He asked)
12. He became a police officer after he graduated from high school. (*reduced clause*)
13. I didn't know you were going to the party, so I didn't offer you a ride. (if)
14. The concert was boring, so we left early. (if)
15. Because she wanted to study Chinese, Melissa went to Beijing for a year. (*reduced clause*)

2 VOCABULARY CHECK

Complete the sentences with the words from the box, making all necessary changes and adding articles (*a/an*) where needed.

aspirations	retain	immersed in	master	pending	monopoly	greedy	renowned
fixture	channel (v)	mediocre	bump into	proficient	carry on	unethical	

1. I'm not very _____ with computers. I only know how to send e-mail and do simple things like that.
2. Some businesses are too _____ for profits. All they care about is money, not their customers.
3. I hadn't talked to Andrea since she changed jobs, but last week I _____ her at a party. It was great to see her.
4. When I was in high school, I had _____ of becoming a professional athlete.
5. Dr. Suarez is _____ psychologist who studies how children learn.
6. I can't believe that Mr. Harris quit his job! He's been _____ in the company for thirty years.
7. It takes a long time to _____ all the techniques of French cooking and become a chef.
8. Cheating on tests is _____. It's not fair to the students who worked hard.
9. In some countries, the government has _____ on tobacco. All tobacco is produced by one national company.
10. In order to _____ the new vocabulary words you learn and not forget them, you need to use them frequently.
11. Loretta is completely _____ her art work. She spends twelve hours a day painting in her studio.
12. I studied Spanish for six months before my trip to Central America, and by the time I got there, I was able to _____ a conversation with people I met.
13. Last year I _____ all my energy into preparing for the university entrance exam.
14. I didn't like that movie very much. I would say it was just _____.
15. A national election is _____. It will take place sometime next year.

3 NOW YOU'RE TALKING!

Situation 2

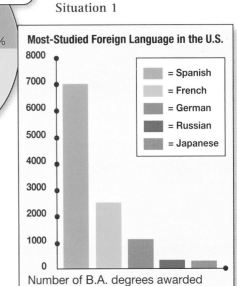

Location of the World's Living Languages

Europe 3%
Americas 15%
Asia 32%
Pacific 19%
Africa 30%

Explain one of these charts to your partner. Describe what each part means and talk about why the information is important.

Situation 1

Most-Studied Foreign Language in the U.S.

= Spanish
= French
= German
= Russian
= Japanese

8000
7000
6000
5000
4000
3000
2000
1000
0

Number of B.A. degrees awarded

You and your partner are talking about your families. Tell your partner about your favorite relative and why he or she is important to you. Ask questions about what your partner tells you.

A Pair work. Look at the pictures and imagine what the people in each situation might say. Briefly review the language notes from Units 4–6 on pages 155–156.

Situation 3

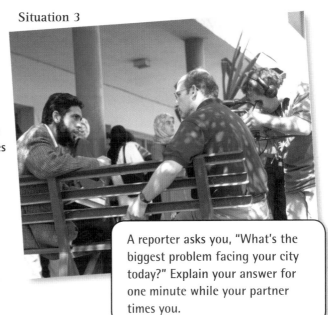

B Pair work. Role-play situations 1, 2, and 3 with a partner. Notice how well you and your partner do the role play. Ask your partner's opinion about your performance.

C Now rate your speaking. Use + for good, ✓ for OK, and – for things you need to improve. Then add two goals for improvement of your speaking.

A reporter asks you, "What's the biggest problem facing your city today?" Explain your answer for one minute while your partner times you.

How did you do?	1	2	3
I was able to express my ideas.			
I spoke easily and fluently, without hesitation.			
I spoke at a good rate of speed—not too fast or too slow.			
I used new vocabulary from the units.			
I used at least three expressions from the units.			
I practiced the grammar from the units.			
Goals for improvement:			
1. _____			
2. _____			

Combo Split A | Advanced

WORLD PASS

Expanding English Fluency

Susan Stempleski
Nancy Douglas
James R. Morgan

Kristin L. Johannsen

THOMSON

Australia · Canada · Mexico · Singapore · Spain · United Kingdom · United States

THOMSON

World Pass Advanced, Combo Split A
Susan Stempleski
Nancy Douglas • James R. Morgan • Kristin L. Johannsen

Publisher: Christopher Wenger
Director of Product Marketing: Amy Mabley
Director of Product Development: Anita Raducanu
Acquisitions Editor: Mary Sutton-Paul
Development Editor: Rebecca Klevberg
Sr. Print Buyer: Mary Beth Hennebury

International Marketing Manager: Ian Martin
Contributing Development Editor: Paul MacIntyre
Compositor: Parkwood Composition Service
Cover Designer: Christopher Hanzie, TYA Inc.

Unit 1   Big Screen, Small Screen

| Unit 1A:
Feature films
2 | **Vocabulary & Expressions:** Movies, p. 2
Grammar: *Such* and *so*, p. 3 |
| Unit 1B:
TV time
4 | **Reading:** The History of Television, p. 4
Writing: The thesis statement, p. 6 |

Unit 2   The World Awaits You

| Unit 2A:
On the road
8 | **Vocabulary & Expressions:** Dazzling destinations, p. 8
Grammar: Past modals, p. 9 |
| Unit 2B:
There and back
10 | **Reading:** Tony Wheeler, Publisher of *Lonely Planet* travel guides, p. 10
Writing: A travel article, p. 12 |

Unit 3   School and Beyond

| Unit 3A:
School life
14 | **Vocabulary & Expressions:** My first year at college, p. 14
Grammar: *Hope* and *wish*, p. 15 |
| Unit 3B:
New school, old school
16 | **Reading:** From Cubicle to Classroom, p. 16
Writing: Advantages and disadvantages of crossover teachers, p. 18 |

Unit 4   Contemporary Issues

| Unit 4A:
In the city
20 | **Vocabulary & Expressions:** Fake merchandise, p. 20
Grammar: Past and present unreal conditionals, p. 21 |
| Unit 4B:
Conflict resolution
22 | **Reading:** Children of the Streets, p. 22
Writing: The opinion essay, p. 23 |

Unit 5   In Other Words

| Unit 5A:
Total immersion
26 | **Vocabulary & Expressions:** What languages are you studying?, p. 26
Grammar: Reduced adverb clauses, p. 27 |
| Unit 5B:
Talk to me.
28 | **Reading:** Studying Spanish in Guatemala, p. 28
Writing: Writing a report, p. 30 |

Unit 6   Ordinary People, Extraordinary Lives

| Lesson A:
Follow your dream!
32 | **Vocabulary & Expressions:** Changing gears, p. 32
Grammar: Reported speech, p. 33 |
| Lesson B:
The kindness of strangers
34 | **Reading:** Lafcadio Hearn, p. 34
Writing: Writing a biography, p. 36 |

Big Screen, Small Screen

Lesson A | Feature films

1 VOCABULARY & EXPRESSIONS

A Complete the sentences with words and expressions from the box, making all necessary changes.

> blockbuster   tearjerker   strike a compromise   wholesome
> B-movie   give away   mainstream

1. I love action movies, but my girlfriend only likes comedies so we always have to _strike a compromise_ when we want to see a film.

2. During the children's hour on TV, the networks broadcast only _wholesome_ educational programs that all ages can watch.

3. I love watching old _B-movies_ with plastic monsters and silly costumes. They're so funny!

4. A _mainstream_ movie is usually very expensive to make, but it is so popular that it makes all the money back and much more besides.

5. Tell me about the new Tom Cruise movie, but don't _give away_ the ending. I'm going to see it with my sister on Friday.

6. A _blockbuster_ movie is a typical movie with famous actors and a somewhat predictable story.

7. I don't understand why people enjoy _tearjerkers_. Real life is full of enough problems—why see movies that make you cry?

B What do you think of these types of movies? Give your response in a complete sentence.

> **Example:** indie movies
> <u>I haven't really seen many of them because they're not really popular in my country.</u>

1. blockbusters

   <u>I don't like blockbuster movies because they're predictable.</u>

2. romantic comedies

   <u>Sometimes it's great to watch romantic comedies.</u>

3. wholesome family movies

   <u>~~It's important~~ The networks broadcast have to advertise when the next ~~how~~ movie isn't appropriated for children.</u>

4. tearjerkers

   <u>I feel stupid when I have to watch that kind of movie.</u>

C When would you say it? Match the expression with the situation.

1. Why do you say that? _D_
2. Can I just say something here? _E_
3. We only have five minutes left. _E_
4. Let's see what someone else has to say. _b_
5. To get back to our topic . . . _F_
6. Sorry, I'm not sure I understand. _A_

     a. to request clarification
     b. to bring other people into a discussion
     c. to bring a discussion to a conclusion
     d. to ask the reason for an opinion
     e. to interrupt in a discussion
     f. to get people to return to the subject

2 GRAMMAR

A Complete the sentences with *so*, *such*, *so much*, or *so many*.

1. I have _____ homework tonight that I'm afraid I can't go to the movie with you. Sorry!

2. My hometown is ____So_____ small that I know everyone there by name.

3. Jenny caught ____Such_____ a bad cold that she had to stay in bed for a week.

4. Yesterday, I got ___So Many_____ e-mail messages that it took me all afternoon to answer them.

5. Andrea speaks English _____So_____ well that many people think she's a native speaker.

6. Jorge has had _____ serious problems with his boss that he's thinking of quitting his job.

7. The dentist said the reason I have _____ terrible teeth is because I eat _____ sugar.

8. That mystery novel was _____So_____ interesting that I stayed up until 4 A.M. reading it.

B Answer the questions using *such* or *so*.

Example: What kind of cook are you?
<u>I'm such a bad cook that my friends won't come to my house for dinner.</u>

1. How much money do some movie stars have?

   _____

2. What kind of teacher did you have for your last English class?

   _____

3. Is it easy to get a driver's license in your country?

   _____

4. Do you have a little or a lot of free time?

   _____

5. How old is the oldest person you've ever talked to?

   _____

6. How many times have you seen your favorite movie?

   _____

7. Did you have a good time on your last birthday?

   _____

8. Was this exercise easy or difficult?

   _____

C Write true sentences about yourself and your interests with these *-ed* and *-ing* adjectives.

1. fascinating _____.

2. disappointed _____.

3. entertaining _____.

4. shocked _____.

5. exciting _____.

Big Screen, Small Screen

Lesson B	TV time

1 READING

A Read the article about the history of television.

The History of Television

1   On January 27, 1926, a group of scientists, including members of Britain's Royal Institution, gathered in a laboratory in an upstairs room in London. **They** were about to witness the world's first television broadcast.

2   The television itself was little more than a collection of old junk taken from discarded machinery: a large cardboard disc with pieces of glass around **it**, behind which were several old electric motors and a mass of glass tubes and other parts from old radio receivers.

3   The engineer who had assembled this device was John Logie Baird, a slim, nervous man in his late thirties, who sat turning the knobs on a small control panel. Seated in the world's first TV studio—a chair in front of the cardboard disc—was a sixteen-year-old boy. You could say **he** was the world's first TV star.

4   As the boy turned his head from side to side, Baird focused and tuned his TV transmitter until the audience could see the image of the boy speaking and moving on a receiver in the same room. Then the audience moved to a separate room, and Baird repeated the demonstration with another receiver **there**—the first actual TV broadcast. To be truthful, the image on the receivers was faint and difficult to see, but Baird's "televisor" showed for the first time that it was possible to send and reproduce live images.

5   In June 1928, Baird transmitted the first outdoor television broadcast, and on August 22 of **the same year**, the General Electric Corporation in the United States produced the first televised news report. It showed the governor of New York accepting the Democratic Party's nomination for president.

6   A number of technical difficulties remained to be worked out, and it was not until 1936 that the first scheduled broadcasting service began. It was produced by the British Broadcasting Corporation in London. In **that same year**, the Radio Corporation of America, which later became RCA Corporation, installed experimental television receivers in 150 New York City homes and began its first transmissions. Their first program was a cartoon called *Felix the Cat*. Three years later, the National Broadcasting Corporation established regular TV broadcasts in the United States. The United States entered World War II in 1941, and broadcasting was suspended until after the war ended in 1945.

7   These first TVs looked very little like the ones we now have. The earliest TVs were large wooden cabinets with screens that measured only 7 to 10 inches (18 to 25 centimeters) diagonally. Today, 27-inch (69-centimeter) screens are very common, and conventional televisions are available with screens as large as 40 inches (100 centimeters). In the 1990s, rear-projection televisions became popular, with screens from 48 inches to 60 inches (122 centimeters to 155 centimeters) diagonally. There are also television sets with screens only 3 inches across—small enough to carry in your pocket.

8   Many of us today would find it difficult to imagine life without television, but the history of **this medium** is not a long one. Will its future development be equally rapid?

B Circle the correct answer.

1. What was John Logie Baird's big achievement?
   a. He produced the first TV show.
   b. He was the first actor on TV.
   c. He built the first working television.
   d. He produced the first news broadcast.

2. Which of these statements about the first television is NOT true?
   a. It was very expensive to build.
   b. Its picture was low in quality.
   c. It was made in England.
   d. It could show motion.

3. Who broadcast the first TV news report?
   a. the British Broadcasting Corporation
   b. John Logie Baird
   c. the General Electric Corporation
   d. the Democratic Party

4. In what year was the public first able to watch TV programs regularly?
   a. 1926
   b. 1928
   c. 1929
   d. 1936

5. What was "televisor" an early word for?
   a. a TV actor
   b. a TV set
   c. a TV announcer
   d. a TV program

6. Where did people watch the first TV broadcast?
   a. in their homes
   b. at the company's office
   c. outdoors
   d. in a laboratory

C Find this information in the reading.

1. the name of an early TV program _____

2. the location of the first TV broadcast _____

3. the largest size of TV screen mentioned _____

4. four things used to build the first TV set _____

_____

D What do these words and phrases in bold refer to?

1. They (par. 1) _____

2. it (par. 2) _____

3. he (par. 3) _____

4. there (par. 4) _____

5. the same year (par. 5) _____

6. that same year (par. 6) _____

7. this medium (par. 8) _____

> **Essays: The thesis statement**
> Every good essay contains a thesis statement, usually in the first paragraph (introduction). The thesis statement is a sentence that expresses the main idea of your essay. It includes the topic as well as your opinion or attitude about the topic. Because it contains an opinion, readers could disagree with it. The essay tells readers why they should agree with this opinion.

A Read these thesis statements. In each one, circle the essay's topic and underline the writer's opinion or attitude toward the topic.

1. Watching television is not a waste of time.

2. Banning cars from the city center would solve many urban problems.

3. My city has some of the world's most interesting tourist attractions.

4. Poor diet is a major cause of many serious health problems.

5. Knowing a foreign language can be a big advantage when looking for a job.

B Are these good thesis statements? Answer *Yes* or *No*.

1. Many movies are produced in Hollywood. _____

2. Too many Hollywood movies today are boring and predictable. _____

3. Movies are a healthy form of escape from everyday stress. _____

4. Kids should be allowed to see any movies they want. _____

5. The three best movies I've seen. _____

6. Hollywood is not the best place for young filmmakers to start their careers. _____

7. I visited Hollywood on a trip to California last year. _____

8. The effects of violent movies on young children. _____

9. The government must do more to support filmmakers in our country. _____

10. I am going to describe my favorite movie. _____

C You are going to write an essay about one of the best (or worst!) movies ever made. First, plan your essay.

Title of movie: _____

Circle: Best / Worst

Thesis statement: _____

_____

Reason 1: _____

Details of Reason 1: _____

_____

_____

Reason 2: _____

Details of Reason 2: _____

_____

_____

D Now write your essay in four paragraphs. Include the thesis statement in the introduction.

Par. 1: Introduction—Introduce the movie and give your opinion.

Par. 2: Discuss the first reason for your opinion.

Par. 3: Discuss the second reason for your opinion.

Par. 4: Conclusion—Should readers see this movie?

UNIT 2

The World Awaits You

Lesson A | On the road

1 VOCABULARY & EXPRESSIONS

A Complete the TV review by filling in each blank with one of the items from the box.

> hypnotic   landscape   atmosphere   household names   relish
> firsthand   take in   guaranteed   relatively   bustling

TV Tonight: *World Wanderers*

The first episode of *World Wanderers* takes us to Norway for a (1)_____ look at the country's beautiful west coast. It starts in the (2)_____ harbor town of Bergen, where we dine at the busy fish market before setting off on a cruise through Norway's world-famous fjords. This is a (3)_____ well-known destination, with hundreds of thousands of visitors every year, but it's still full of surprises. The unique (4)_____ of mountains that rise straight up from the sea is truly (5)_____. It's a lot to (6)_____. The only negative point about the show is it's just thirty minutes, too short to really (7)_____ everything we're seeing. But the producers do a good job of conveying the (8)_____ of each place we visit.

In the future, the show promises a mix of destinations—from (9)_____, like Paris and the Pyramids of Egypt, to new discoveries, like the Indonesian island of Lombok. It's (10)_____ to make you want to take a trip!

B Complete the sentences using your own ideas.

1. To me, _____ is <u>priceless</u> because _____
_____.

2. Sometimes I feel <u>powerless</u> about _____ because
_____.

3. Asking "_____?" is a <u>meaningless</u> question because
_____.

4. For me, _____ sometimes feels <u>effortless</u> because _____
_____.

C Read the phone conversation and complete the expressions.

Operator: Thank you for calling Golden Tours. How (1)_____ I (2)_____ your call?

Rafael: I'd like some information about your tours to Hawaii.

Operator: One (3)_____, please.

Agent: Good afternoon, (4)_____ is Wayne. (5)_____ may I (6)_____ you?

Rafael: Could you please (7)_____ me the (8)_____ of the tour to Hawaii that was in your newspaper ad?

Agent: Prices start at just $3,000.

Rafael: Oh . . . I'm (9)_____ that's a little (10)_____ of my price range.

Agent: In that case, you might be interested in one of our budget tours. We offer . . .

2 GRAMMAR

A Match each sentence with the function of the underlined past modal phrase.

1. You <u>must have</u> spent a lot of time in England because you have a British accent. _____
2. I <u>shouldn't have</u> eaten the whole cake. I feel sick! _____
3. I <u>could have</u> cooked something for dinner, but we decided to go out for pizza. _____
4. Jessica <u>might have</u> forgotten that we have a meeting now. _____
5. I <u>would have</u> helped you with your computer, but you didn't ask me. _____
6. Frank <u>couldn't have</u> written this report all by himself. It's 200 pages! _____
7. You <u>should have</u> called me on my cell phone instead of keeping me waiting. _____

a. making a strong suggestion in the past
b. expressing willingness in the past
c. making a conclusion about past events
d. expressing possibility in the past
e. talking about a possible explanation
f. expressing impossibility in the past
g. expressing regret about a past action that was taken

B Rewrite each sentence using a past modal phrase.

1. I was willing to give you a ride to the party, but I didn't know you were going.

   _____.

2. It's possible that you left your dictionary on the train.

   _____.

3. It was a very bad idea for Carla to speak to her boss that way.

   _____.

4. I was probably taking a shower when you called because I didn't hear the phone.

   _____.

5. It's not possible that Eric forgot about our date.

   _____.

6. It was a good idea to review the vocabulary words before the test, but you didn't do it.

   _____.

C Write true sentences about yourself using past modal phrases.

1. Write about a bad decision you made. (should have)

   _____

2. Write about something you lost. What happened? (might have)

   _____

3. Write about something that was possible in the past that you didn't try. (could have)

   _____

4. Write about something you regret doing. (shouldn't have)

   _____

The World Awaits You

Lesson B	There and back

1 READING

A Read this article about the founder of a travel guide company.

Travel Profile: Tony Wheeler, Publisher of *Lonely Planet* Travel Guides

1   When Tony Wheeler was ten years old, his parents asked him what he would like for a Christmas present. He asked for two things: a globe and a filing cabinet. Both were appropriate gifts for a boy who would grow up to head the world's largest travel publisher.

2   Today, Wheeler's company, *Lonely Planet* Publications, produces more than 650 different titles, covering destinations form Australia to Zimbabwe. Over six million copies annually are sold in 118 countries around the world. In other words, one in every four English-language guidebooks sold is a *Lonely Planet* guide.

3   In the early 1970s, Wheeler was a young engineer in England when he decided to take time off and see the world. He and his wife, Maureen, set off to travel through Asia to Australia, making the entire trip overland. When they reached Sydney, after nine months on the road, they found themselves **barraged** with the same questions over and over again: What kind of transportation did you use? What places did you take in? How much did it cost? Finally, Tony sat down at his kitchen table and wrote a ninety-four-page **pamphlet,** which he called "Across Asia on the Cheap." It gave details for the route they traveled from Europe across Turkey, Afghanistan, and India through to Australia. The Wheelers published it themselves, and were surprised and pleased when 8,500 copies were sold in bookstores across Australia.

4   From the sales of their book, the Wheelers earned enough money to spend another year traveling in Asia. At the end of 1974, they rented a room in an old **fleabag** hotel in Singapore and spent three months writing "South-East Asia on a Shoestring." The "yellow Bible" was an instant success; and after twelve editions, its cover is still yellow. When their India guidebook was published in 1980, it sold 100,000 copies, and the Wheelers found themselves heading a major business **enterprise**.

5   Surprisingly, Wheeler still spends a lot of time on the road, traveling and doing firsthand research for new guidebooks. Over 120 writers actually produce the books, but Wheeler himself relishes staying involved. Last year, he traveled to Shanghai, Singapore, Finland, the Baltic countries, Poland, Italy, Switzerland, Germany, Iceland, and Japan. He even found time to take a multicountry safari in Africa.

6   "I still do some writing every year," he says. "I've been involved in a couple of writing projects recently. More of the travel, though, is because I want to go to places, and there are things I want to see. We call it 'quality control,' just taking the books and trying them out."

7   Wheeler has been traveling since a **tender age**. His father was an airport manager for a British aviation company, and every few years the family was posted to a new country. They lived in Pakistan, the Bahamas, Canada, the United States, and England. Because he seldom spent two years at the same school, young Tony grew accustomed to being a foreigner.

8   After thirty years in the business, Wheeler admits that the *Lonely Planet* guidebooks have changed **drastically**. "When we started we were in our early twenties and writing books for people also in their early twenties, who were penniless. Now the business is so much bigger—there are so many more people traveling. Travel is now thought of more as something that's a right rather than a privilege."

9   Wheeler still strives to raise awareness of the effects that travel has on the world. "There's no question that tourism can be damaging on all sorts of levels. I think that people involved in the industry and those traveling have to be very aware of that and act accordingly. Although it is an activity that's sustainable, we have to think very carefully about how to make it work."

B Write the paragraph number next to the description.

1. Most recent trips _____

2. Wheeler's philosophy of tourism _____

3. How *Lonely Planet* became a success _____

4. The Wheelers' first publication _____

5. An international childhood _____

6. Why Wheeler still travels _____

7. Facts about *Lonely Planet* _____

8. A boy with big dreams _____

9. How the guidebooks are different now _____

C Locate this information in the reading.

1. Wheeler's original occupation _____

2. The number of *Lonely Planet* guidebooks sold every year _____

3. Two cities that Wheeler visited last year _____

4. The title of the Wheelers' first guide _____

5. The year they produced a guidebook to India _____

6. An Asian country where Wheeler lived as a child _____

7. The number of writers that *Lonely Planet* employs _____

8. The number of different books that *Lonely Planet* publishes _____

D Find the meaning of the boldfaced items in the reading from their context.

1. A **pamphlet** is ___.

   a. a short book   b. a kind of magazine   c. a map

2. A **fleabag** hotel is ___.

   a. very luxurious   b. cheap and uncomfortable   c. in the jungle

3. If someone is at a **tender age**, they are ___.

   a. young   b. middle-aged   c. elderly

4. A business **enterprise** is ___.

   a. an executive   b. a regulation   c. a company

5. If you are **barraged** with questions, people ask you ___.

   a. rudely   b. many times   c. gently

6. If something changes **drastically**, the change is ___.

   a. extreme   b. slow   c. unimportant

A Read this article that was submitted to a student travel magazine. The mistakes have been underlined. Mark the type of mistake above each one, using the symbols in the box.

Sp	spelling	VT	verb tense
WF	word form	WW	wrong word
P	punctuation	WO	word order
X	word(s) missing	??	I don't understand this.

Too many visitors to South Korea spend all of their time in Seoul. In order to really understand my country's culture and four thousand **(1)** <u>year</u> of history, you **(2)** <u>had better</u> visit the city of Gyeongju.

Gyeongju **(3)** _____ which is located in the southern part of the country, was the **(4)** <u>cappitol</u> of the ancient kingdom of Silla for almost a thousand years. It was the center of the arts, science, and government in a very **(5)** <u>wealth</u> country. In the Gyeongju National Museum you **(6)** <u>would</u> see the gold crowns of the Silla kings and queens and learn about the people's comfortable way of life.

In many ways, Gyeongju is **(7)** <u>likes</u> an open-air museum. All around the city, there are ancient palaces and temples. The kings and queens of Silla are **(8)** <u>bury</u> in huge tombs that look like hills covered with green grass. Just outside of the city is a mountain called Namsan. The forest there is filled with ancient statues and temples, and you can spend days just hiking in it. Tourists can also rent bicycles to ride through the countryside and visit more **(9)** <u>sites ancient</u>. One of **(10)** _____ most beautiful is Seokguram, a statue of the Buddha built inside a stone cave.

Visitors who come to Gyeongju will see a different side of Korea. Today, it's a modern country, but you will soon see why Gyeongju was called the "City of Gold" long ago.

B Correct each of the mistakes in the article.

1. _____ 6. _____
2. _____ 7. _____
3. _____ 8. _____
4. _____ 9. _____
5. _____ 10. _____

C Now write your own travel article about a destination that visitors to your country will enjoy. Include an introduction to attract your readers' interest, one or two body paragraphs of information about the destination, and a conclusion that pulls the article together.

School and Beyond

Lesson A | School life

1 VOCABULARY & EXPRESSIONS

A Match these words and phrases with their meanings.

1. sleep deprivation _K_
2. stick to _B_
3. hectic _A_
4. cope with _D_
5. bond with _H_
6. mishap _J_
7. rash _G_
8. compulsory _____
9. apprehensive _F_
10. sign up for _C_
11. expectation _E_

a. hurried, excessively busy
b. follow a plan or a promise
c. register yourself, enroll
d. deal successfully with a difficult situation
e. what you believe or hope will happen
f. nervous or fearful
g. sudden, without proper planning
h. form a close relationship with someone
i. required for everyone
j. minor accident without serious results
k. feeling extremely tired from lack of rest

B Complete the sentences with the correct form of a word from the box. Use each word only once.

| accept | except | pass | past | lose |
| advise | advice | affect | effect | loose |

1. I went on a diet and lost fifteen pounds, and now I have to buy a lot of new clothes. My favorite jeans are too ___LOOSE___ to wear!

2. Jameela applied to four different universities, and she was ___ACCEPTED___ at all of them. Now she faces a tough decision.

3. The topic of my essay is the negative ___effect___ of smoking on health.

4. My professor ___ADVISE___ me to take a special course this summer.

5. Jason ___PASSED___ his driving test the first time he took it, and now he's driving his parents' car everywhere.

6. Min-Chul spent the ___PAST___ year studying for his university entrance exam.

7. I'm really enjoying all of my classes, ___EXCEPT___ biology. I'm not very interested in science.

8. I think you really should quit your part-time job. Working at night is starting to ___AFFECT___ your grades.

9. I can never remember where I put my cell phone. I ___LOSE___ it at least once a day!

10. This book contains a lot of good ___ADVICES___ on how to improve your English fluency.

C Imagine you're at an interview. Write one phrase could you use in each situation.

1. The interviewer asks a question, and you need to think about your answer.

_____.

2. You're not sure what the interviewer meant in a question.

_____.

3. You're not satisfied with your answer, and you want to say it differently.

_____.

2 GRAMMAR

A Fill in the correct form of the verb. Some are negative.

1. Your new cell phone has really small keys. Do you wish you _____ (buy) it?

2. On exam day, a lot of students wish they _____ (study) harder.

3. My brother lives overseas. I really wish you _____ (meet) him.

4. Eva wishes she _____ (find) a better job soon because her salary is very low.

5. I got angry at my boyfriend last night, and now I really wish I _____ (say) such mean things to him.

6. Luis wishes the other students in the dorm _____ (be) quieter. They listen to loud music almost every night.

7. It's raining harder now. I wish I _____ (bring) my umbrella.

8. Alex was absent yesterday. The teacher wishes he _____ (miss) class.

9. I wish I _____ (be) so sleepy in the morning. I often miss the bus and get to class late.

10. Yong-min has to work late tonight. I wish he _____ (go) to the movie with us.

B Write sentences about your own wishes and hopes for these things.

1. your English class _____.

_____.

2. your city _____.

_____.

3. the environment _____.

_____.

4. future technology _____.

_____.

C Fill in the spaces with the correct form of a verb from the box.

> hope   wish   make   allow   let

1. When I was a child, my parents always _____ me finish my homework before watching TV.

2. I really _____ we'll have good weather for our trip to the beach this weekend.

3. I think teachers should _____ us to use our dictionaries when we take an exam.

4. My neighbor plays the piano really badly. I _____ he would take some lessons!

5. My boss _____ me take a day off on Monday because I worked on the weekend.

6. In my opinion, you shouldn't _____ children eat foods they don't like.

7. Carla bought a desktop computer, but now she really _____ she had gotten a laptop.

8. No dogs are _____ in any of the city parks.

School and Beyond

1 READING

A Read this article about crossover teachers.

From **Cubicle** to Classroom

June Diaz had it all. She enjoyed her work as a public relations specialist at Arrow Communications, a firm in Miami. She had been with her company for almost ten years, and she had received several promotions during that time. Her clients loved the magazines and reports she produced for them. But, somehow, she just couldn't get an old dream out of her head.

"I always wanted to be a teacher," she says. "When I was a little kid, I used to play school with all my friends. I stood in front and made them recite their lessons." In high school, she started a volunteer tutoring service to help elementary school kids in low-income neighborhoods with their homework. But, when she started college, her parents talked her out of majoring in education, saying there was "no money in it." Instead, she earned a business degree. "I wish I hadn't listened," she says today.

Today, Diaz is following her dream. She enrolled last year in a special program at Atlantic Coastal University that allows professionals to become teachers in only a year by taking special courses. She is one of a growing number of "crossover teachers" in the United States—people who have left their former careers to go into the classroom. Among them are nurses who became science teachers and office managers who teach math. According to the National Center for Education Information in Washington, over 200,000 new teachers were trained in this type of program in the first six years the courses were offered.

In the past, regulations about who could teach in America's public schools were much more **rigid.** Only graduates with a four-year degree in education could qualify, and candidates had to go through a lengthy **bureaucratic** process of certification. But in the 1980s, many cities were experiencing a **drastic** shortage of teachers, and they began looking for new ways to **recruit** people who truly wanted to teach. Programs to train crossover teachers have helped ease the shortage.

Daniel Feldstein was the supervisor of public schools in New York City, one of the first cities to hire crossover teachers. "These are people who believe teaching is a calling," he says. "It's not just a job. They're incredibly dedicated." He says that students really enjoy having teachers with a broad experience of the world—someone who has had another career before coming to the classroom.

Not everyone supports the idea, however. "These crossover teachers have far less training than their colleagues do," points out Lauretta Coggs, president of the National Association of Teachers. "And when they are forty years old, they may have only one or two years of teaching experience compared with a professional teacher who has already been in the classroom for almost twenty years. There's no substitute for experience."

Some parents also express doubts about this new **breed** of teachers. "My son's social studies teacher used to be a banker," says Natalia Chen. "I'm sure he knows a lot about money, but does he really know how kids learn best?"

It's not easy becoming a crossover teacher. Most continue to work at their **previous** jobs while taking courses, resulting in hectic schedules. After completing part of their course work, they also do practice teaching, working in an actual classroom supervised by an experienced teacher. This requires **candidates** to arrange for one day off from work at their regular job every week.

Diaz recently had her first day of practice teaching, working with second graders at a nearby elementary school. "I'm teaching reading and math. I'm having the time of my life, and I haven't even graduated yet!"

B Read the statements and circle *T* for *true*, *F* for *false*, or *NI* for *no information*. Change the false sentences to make them true.

1. Crossover teachers must study for four years to become qualified.   T   F   NI

2. In high school, June Diaz started a tutoring service.   T   F   NI

3. June Diaz earned a bachelor's degree in education.   T   F   NI

4. June Diaz was unhappy with her job at Arrow Communications.   T   F   NI

5. People from different fields have become crossover teachers.   T   F   NI

6. Many American states have a problem with too many qualified teachers.   T   F   NI

7. The number of crossover teachers is falling.   T   F   NI

8. Most parents accept the idea of crossover teachers.   T   F   NI

9. June Diaz has already started teaching.   T   F   NI

10. New York was one of the first cities to hire crossover teachers.   T   F   NI

11. Teachers in the United States all have the same kind of training.   T   F   NI

12. June Diaz plans to get a job in an elementary school.   T   F   NI

C Answer in your own words.

1. What are crossover teachers? _____.

_____.

2. How do people become crossover teachers? _____.

_____.

3. Why do people become crossover teachers? _____.

_____.

4. Who supports this program? Why? _____.

_____.

5. Who disagrees with this program? Why? _____.

_____.

D Find the boldfaced words in the reading with these meanings. (Hint: There is one in the title).

1. involving complicated official rules _____

2. earlier _____

3. type or kind _____

4. people who are trying for a position _____

5. a small section of an office, for one person _____

6. strict and unchanging _____

7. severe, serious _____

8. find and hire people for a job _____

A You are going to write an opinion essay about the advantages and disadvantages of crossover teachers. Reread the article on page 16.

B List these ideas in the correct column. Add as many others as you can to each column—both ideas from the reading and your own ideas.

have less training
are very enthusiastic
can be hired quickly

Advantages of Crossover Teachers

Disadvantages of Crossover Teachers

C Plan and write your opinion essay about crossover teachers, using information from the article and ideas you listed in the chart above.

Par. 1: Introduction—What are crossover teachers?

Par. 2: Advantages of crossover teachers

Par. 3: Disadvantages of crossover teachers

Par. 4: Conclusion—Are crossover teachers a good idea for your country? Why, or why not?

Contemporary Issues

Lesson A | In the city

1 VOCABULARY & EXPRESSIONS

A Read the article on illegal brand-name copying and fill in the spaces with the correct form of a word or expression from the box.

> mediocre   panic   monopoly   greedy   compensate
> crack down   take to court   pending   consumer   churn out
> rip off   unauthorized   emerging

Last week, the government announced that it was (1) _CRACKING DOWN_ on manufacturers who produce (2) _UNAUTHORIZED_ copies of brand-name fashions such as shoes, bags, and watches. The announcement caused (3) _PANIC_ among many small shopkeepers in Central Market. One manufacturer of fake luxury brand name watches has already been (4) _TAKEN TO COURT_, and several other cases are (5) _PENDING_, with decisions expected soon.

The makers of genuine fashion products believe that they should be (6) _COMPENSATED_ for the money they have lost to illegal manufacturers. "These illegal manufacturers must not be allowed to (7) _RIP OFF_ millions of copies of the designs that we work so hard to produce," says James Torres, president of the Fashion Industry Council. "It's especially a problem for (8) _EMERGING_ designers who are just starting out in the field. Furthermore, the quality of these products is (9) _MEDIOCRE_, and it gives the public a bad impression."

(10) _CONSUMERS_ who shop for brand-name fashions have different opinions. Some support the government's campaign. "Dishonest stores can (11) _CHURN OUT_ customers by selling them fake merchandise," says Lori Miller. But Josh Richards disagrees with the campaign. "The real problem is that these fashion companies are too (12) _GREEDY_ for money and fame. They have a (13) _MONOPOLY_ on their business so they can charge any crazy price they want."

B Match the parts of these expressions for giving your opinion.

1. Without _E_   a. that, but
2. Take _F_   b. besides
3. Not to mention _D_   c. an idea
4. I'm _G_   d. the fact that
5. To give you _C_   e. a doubt
6. Not only _A_   f. for example
7. And _B_   g. convinced that

A Complete each sentence with a clause from the box.

1. If I weren't so tired, _I would go to Leslie's party tonight_.
2. If I hadn't had an exam the next day, _I wouldn't need to go today_.
3. If I ate breakfast, _I wouldn't be so hungry in class_.
4. If I hadn't studied so much, _I wouldn't have gotten such a good grade_.
5. If I had left earlier, _I wouldn't have missed my bus_.
6. If I had gone to the store last night, _I would have gone to the movie with you_.
7. If I had a day off, _I would sleep until noon_.

I wouldn't be so hungry in class	I would sleep until noon	I wouldn't need to go today
I would go to Leslie's party tonight	I wouldn't have gotten such a good grade	
I would have gone to the movie with you	I wouldn't have missed my bus	

B Which sentences in Activity A are about the present? _1, 2, 3, 7_

Which sentences in Activity A are about the past? _4, 5, 6_

C Fill in the correct form of each verb. All are unreal situations in the past.

1. If I (know) _knew_ you were sick last week, I (visit) _would have visited_ you.
2. We (go) _would have gone_ with you to the theme park on Saturday if we (have) _had had_ enough money.
3. If Beth (not study) _doesn't study_ all night, she (not pass) _won't pass_ her computer programming test.
4. You (meet) _would have meet_ my new boyfriend if you (come) _had come_ to the party last weekend.
5. If you (listen) _had listen_ to your friends' advice, you (not have) _wouldn't have_ so many problems.
6. Marianne (go) _would have gone_ to National University if she (get) _had gotten_ a better score on the entrance exam.
7. I (send) _would have send_ you a postcard from Australia if you (give) _had ~~not~~ give_ me your address!

D Write your own sentences about the results of these unreal situations.

1. (you started learning English at two years of age)

I would be fluent on English if I had started learning it at two years of age.

2. (you were the oldest/youngest/only child in your family)

If I were the youngest child on my family, I would be more calm then I'm now.

School and Beyond

Lesson B	Conflict resolution

A Read this article about the problem of homeless children.

Children of the Streets

Homeless people are a tragic sight in the cities of nearly every country in the world, but the ones in the most difficult situation are the street children. Today, at least fifty million children struggle to survive without a home or parents to support them. No one knows the exact number of homeless children, because they often fear and avoid authorities. Some have run away from home because of family problems, while others have been forced to leave home because their parents simply lacked enough money to support them. They manage to survive through hard work, luck, and courage. Here are the stories of three street children.

Dolgion is fourteen years old. He lives in Ulaanbaatar, the capital of the central Asian country Mongolia. When he was seven, his family's home burned down, and they were forced to move in with relatives. His mother left to find work in another city, and then one day his father disappeared. Finally, Dolgion was asked to leave because his relatives couldn't afford to feed him. Since then, he has made his home with a group of other street children in an underground hole for heating pipes. During the day, they collect empty bottles to sell, and together they earn about two dollars a day. If there's any leftover money after they buy noodles for their evening meal, they spend it playing computer games in a PC game room. His dreams? "When I grow up," he says, "I will own a bottle-collection point. And I will find my parents. I will buy a house, and we will all live together."

Rukshana and her little sister sleep under a bridge in Mumbai, India. Rukshana, who is fifteen, tries to earn enough money to support both of them so that eleven-year-old Deepa will be able to go to school. Every morning during rush hour, she boards the commuter trains from the suburbs to the central city and spends the entire day selling hair ornaments and magazines to women traveling to work. If the police catch her, she will have to pay a fine—more money than she earns in a week. The girls' parents both died several years ago, and their older brother lives in a faraway village and has five children of his own that he struggles to support. But, their life is not all hardship. At least three times a week, the two sisters go to see a movie—they especially love family dramas. In the future, Rukshana wants learn to read and write. "Then I will get a proper house—make something of my life and show people. I will have some gold jewelry of my own. Then my life will be stable."

Jack, who is only twelve, and looks even younger, is a tiny, thin boy with tired eyes. He earns his living by cleaning passengers' shoes on public transportation in the streets of Manila. It's exhausting work, and he earns only three dollars a day. "I don't know how many shoes I have to wipe to earn it," he says. "I get kicked on my back by some of the passengers." On days he is unable to earn enough money this way, he is forced to beg in the park where he sleeps. Jack was forced to leave the home he shared with his mother, brothers, and sisters in order to earn a living. He misses them terribly and hopes to be reunited with them. He likes to draw pictures when he can't express his feelings in words: "This house is for me and my brothers and sisters," he says. "Some of them would study, and some would guard the house. That's the kind of life I want to have."

B Complete the chart with information from the reading. Write short notes, not complete sentences.

	Dolgion	Rukshana	Jack
Age			
Country			
Family Background			
Reason for Homelessness			
How They Support Themselves			
Future Hopes			

C Answer the questions.

1. What obstacles do these children face? _____
   _____
   _____.

2. Do you think any of these children will achieve their dreams? _____ Why, or why not? _____
   _____
   _____.

3. What surprised you in this article? _____
   _____
   _____.

> When writing about your opinion, you should support your argument with details and facts, in order to persuade your readers to agree with your opinion.

A Read each opinion. Mark the statement that does NOT support the opinion.

1. University students should be allowed to choose all of their courses, without requirements.

   _____ a. Students are all individuals with their own needs and interests.

   _____ b. One program can't meet the needs of every student.

   _____ c. A modern university offers a tremendous variety of courses.

2. Nuclear power plants are not a good energy option for the future.

   _____ a. Many countries have stopped building new nuclear power plants.

   _____ b. Their cost is very high in comparison with other ways to produce electricity.

   _____ c. There is a possibility of devastating accidents if they malfunction.

3. Free music downloads from the Internet bring more benefits than problems.

   _____ a. They give emerging musicians a chance to reach new audiences.

   _____ b. Consumers often find new music that they enjoy and will later buy it.

   _____ c. This practice is unfair to artists, who have to work hard to earn a living.

4. Parents need to control the amount of time that their children spend online.

   _____ a. Kids who don't get enough outdoor play easily become overweight.

   _____ b. Children become socially isolated if they spend all their time with online friends.

   _____ c. The cost of a new computer is far too high for many families in this country.

5. The manufacture and sale of cigarettes should be banned in this country.

   _____ a. Last year, over 50,000 citizens died from diseases caused by smoking.

   _____ b. Two of the largest companies in the country are cigarette producers.

   _____ c. Precious farmland is wasted on production of a crop that actually harms people.

B Complete each of these statements by circling your opinion. Then give three reasons to support this opinion.

1. Students in our country (should/should not) be required to learn a foreign language in high school.

   a. _____

   b. _____

   c. _____

2. There (should/should not) be a law requiring people to wear their seat belts in cars.

   a. _____

   b. _____

   c. _____

3. Our country (should/should not) encourage more foreign tourists to come here.

   a. _____

   b. _____

   c. _____

C Write short replies to these two messages, agreeing or disagreeing with them. Be sure to support your opinion with reasons.

City Beat

What's the best thing about urban life? The worst? Post your thoughts here or respond to writers who have already said how they feel.

I've lived in a big city for six months now, and what strikes me the most is how rude people are! I live in an apartment building, and I always say "Hello" to the neighbors I see when I pick up my mail. They just nod at me and then head for the elevator. No one in the city ever holds the door open when you have your hands full of packages, no one is friendly when you go into a store, and everybody walks down the street yelling into their cell phones. I'll never get used to this kind of behavior. At least I hope not!—Frankie79

_____
_____
_____
_____
_____
_____
_____
_____
_____

The thing that I enjoy the most about major cities is that you can do anything you want, any time you want. Some of the biggest stores here don't close until midnight, and the small ones are open by 6 A.M. You can do your grocery shopping on New Year's Day if you like because all the supermarkets are open. In the town where I grew up, the streets were dead quiet after 7 P.M., so I love all the noise and activity of the city. I think it's just great that everything is open almost all the time.—Moonlight22

_____
_____
_____
_____
_____
_____
_____
_____
_____

In Other Words

1 VOCABULARY & EXPRESSIONS

A Form sentences by matching the columns to show the meaning of the underlined words.

1. If you <u>convey</u> an idea, _____   a. you don't forget them.

2. If you are <u>proficient</u> in a language, _____   b. you listen to and respond to another person.

3. If you speak in <u>halting</u> way, _____   c. you learned it when you were a baby.

4. If you are <u>immersed</u> in a language, _____   d. you speak it very well.

5. If Arabic is your <u>primary language</u>, _____   e. you communicate it to another person.

6. If your English is <u>passable</u>, _____   f. you practice it after not using it for a long time.

7. If you <u>brush up on</u> your French, _____   g. you speak it the best of all your languages.

8. If you <u>carry on</u> a conversation, _____   h. you speak slowly with many mistakes.

9. If Spanish is your <u>mother tongue</u>, _____   i. you are in contact with it all day.

10. If you <u>master</u> Russian, _____   j. you learn to speak it very well.

11. If you <u>retain</u> new words, _____   k. you speak it fairly well.

B Answer the questions with your own ideas.

1. What do you do to <u>retain</u> new vocabulary words? _____

_____

2. What are some situations where people are <u>immersed</u> in a foreign language? _____

_____

3. How long would it take a foreign student to become <u>proficient</u> in your language? _____

_____

4. What are some good ways to <u>brush up on</u> a language you studied a long time ago? _____

_____

C Review the meanings of these acronyms and initialisms on page 53 of your Student Book. Then use them to complete the sentences.

> PIN   ASAP   AC   ATM   TBA   TGIF

1. We're having a _____ party after work at Sal's Pizza. Want to join us?

2. You shouldn't write your _____ number down because someone could find it and use it to access your bank account.

3. Could you turn the _____ on? It's really hot in here.

4. This form is very important. You need to fill it in and submit it _____.

5. We still don't know the time and place for the job interviews. They are _____.

6. I'll stop by the _____ on the way home from work and get some cash.

2 GRAMMAR

A Reduce the adverb clauses in these sentences.

1. Because she was interested in Chinese culture, Nina decided to study Mandarin.
   Being interested in Chinese culture, Nina decided to study Mandarin.

2. Since she had never studied a foreign language before, she didn't realize it was supposed to be difficult.
   _____.

3. She went to her Mandarin class every night after she finished work.
   _____.

4. Because she learned five new words every day, she soon developed a large vocabulary.
   _____.

5. After she had studied for two years, she took a trip to Beijing.
   _____.

6. Because she was able to carry on a conversation, she really enjoyed her time in China.
   _____.

B Combine the pairs of sentences with a reduced adverbial clause, using the word in parenthesis.

1. He took classes at night. He worked in a factory during the day. (while)
   While taking classes at night, he worked in a factory during the day.

2. We started this course. We've learned a lot of new vocabulary. (since)
   _____.

3. She graduated from college. She went to work for an airline. (after)
   _____.

4. I take a bath and brush my teeth. I go to bed. (before)
   _____.

C Are these sentences with reduced adverb clauses correct? Mark each one *C* for *correct* or *I* for *incorrect*. Rewrite the incorrect ones to make them logical.

Example: While walking on the beach, the waves were very big after the storm. _I_
While walking on the beach, I saw big waves after the storm.

1. Having been burned in a fire, the doctors treated the victim in the hospital. _____
   _____.

2. After leaving the office, Carla went to the post office to buy some stamps. _____
   _____.

3. Not wearing a coat, I felt very cold all day. _____
   _____.

4. Using a microscope, the deadly bacteria were easy to see. _____
   _____.

5. Riding my bicycle, a car swerved in front of me. _____
   _____.

6. Barking happily, Kevin played with his dog. _____
   _____.

In Other Words

1 READING

A Read this article about a language-learning experience

Studying Spanish in Guatemala
by Johanna Kristiansen

Can animals think? I had to **consider** this a moment before answering. "Sí, creo que . . ."

Not your typical Spanish class topic, but this was not your typical Spanish class. My teacher and I sat at a table on a rooftop terrace, looking out over the city of Quetzaltenango, Guatemala. At the next table, another teacher and student were talking about recipes. This was only my second week of study.

I had come to Guatemala at the beginning of a trip through Central America, hoping to brush up on my college Spanish. I had plenty of company. Guatemala's dozens of Spanish language schools, some of the best and most inexpensive anywhere, draw students from around the world.

Though there are schools throughout the country, most are in two cities—Antigua and Quetzaltenango. Deciding to split my time between the two, I went first to Antigua, the old capital, which is a handsome city of colonial streets lined with brown and yellow houses. The city is surrounded by tall blue volcanoes, which erupt every few centuries.

It's not surprising that over 12,000 foreigners every year come to study in Antigua's language schools. Enrollment is simple and **straightforward.** One Saturday afternoon, I strolled into the office of a school that had been recommended to me, and on Monday morning, I began classes.

My teacher, Juan Cecilio, was incredibly patient with my halting Spanish. Seeing that I had forgotten the basics, he gave me a fast review of Spanish grammar in only five days. By the end of the week, we were talking (slowly) about Guatemalan history and the cost of living.

All of Antigua's schools follow a similar system. Students have four hours of **one-on-one** instruction with a teacher every morning. Afternoons are for extra lessons, sightseeing, or hanging out in the town's cafés. Classes run from Monday to Friday, and students have the **option** to change teachers each week.

Like most students, I chose homestay accommodation. My hosts, Luis and Angelina, had both lived in the United States, but our conversations were entirely in Spanish. Dinners with them were a great way to practice the language, and I learned about aspects of Guatemalan life that are invisible to the average tourist.

Quetzaltenango was a complete contrast. Usually called by its local name, Xela (shay-la), it is a busy commercial center, not a living museum. Many Spanish schools there sponsor community projects, such as schools and clinics, in the surrounding countryside. Casa Xelaju, where I studied, has tutoring programs for children in a nearby village, and many students volunteer.

Xela has three universities, and many of the city's Spanish teachers hold teaching degrees from one of them. Flori, the teacher I talked with on the rooftop, was a graduate in Spanish and history. By this time, I could **handle** some fairly complex topics, and our talks ranged from astrology to names of vegetables.

The best part of one-on-one teaching is that the daily lesson can be about anything you want. One day, another student and I asked our teachers to come with us to the Mayan market in a small village nearby. Together, the four of us asked questions and learned about the uses of the **medicinal** plants on sale and the **significance** of the traditional weaving designs.

Though most students stay for several months, every Friday afternoon is "graduation day" for those who are leaving, with a party and a cake. On the day I left Xela, several long-term students gave **tearful** goodbye speeches, telling moving stories of their volunteer work with village kids and good times with their host families. For now, I could only thank my teachers for helping me to put my thoughts into Spanish words—but in the back of my mind, I was already planning how to come back and really master the language.

B Find this information in the reading.

1. Which cities did the author study in? _____

2. Where had she studied Spanish before? _____

3. Why did she want to improve her Spanish? _____
   _____.

4. How many students are in each class? _____

5. How many hours per week do students have class? _____

6. Where do students stay? _____

7. Who chooses the topics of the lessons? _____

8. What other activities can students do? _____
   _____.

C Match the boldfaced words from the story with their meanings.

1. consider _____   a. without problems

2. medicinal _____   b. cope with

3. tearful _____   c. choice, possibility

4. significance _____   d. sad

5. handle _____   e. think carefully about

6. one-on-one _____   f. individual

7. option _____   g. useful for treating disease

8. straightforward _____   h. meaning, importance

D Give your opinion.

1. What are some good points of learning a language this way? _____
   _____.

2. What are some bad points? _____
   _____.

3. Would you like to take a language course like this? Why, or why not? _____
   _____.

A Study these charts and write a paragraph explaining the information in each one. Review the expressions on page 56 in your Student Book.

1.

First language vocabulary by child's age

Number of words (y-axis): 0, 100, 200, 300, 400, 500, 600, 700, 800, 900, 1000, 1100, 1200

Age in years (x-axis): 1.5, 2, 2.5, 3, 3.5, 4

2.

Number of Internet Users by Language

(y-axis): 0, 50,000,000, 100,000,000, 150,000,000, 200,000,000, 250,000,000, 300,000,000

Language	Value
English	291
Chinese	113
Japanese	67
Spanish	56
German	54

3.

Primary languages in Malaysia

- English 5%
- Indian 10%
- Chinese 25%
- Malay 60%

_____
_____
_____
_____
_____
_____
_____
_____
_____
_____
_____
_____
_____
_____

B Write a report about opportunities for students in your country to practice their English. Divide your report into sections and give each one a heading. Your report should answer these questions.

1. Overall, do students have enough opportunities to practice their English?

2. What opportunities do students have to practice listening and speaking?

3. What opportunities do students have to practice reading and writing?

4. What recommendations do you have for providing more opportunities for students?

1 VOCABULARY & EXPRESSIONS

A Complete the sentences with the correct form of a word or expression from the box.

> sidetracked   storied   juggling   channel   have something in mind
> cause a stir   aspirations   twinkle   bump into   renowned
> swap   fixture   apprentice

1. Single parents have to be experts at _____ their work and family responsibilities.

2. Dale worked as an _____ to a carpenter before he started his own construction business.

3. Dr. Clark is one the most _____ historians in our country.

4. When I was young, I had _____ of being an astronaut when I grew up.

5. Kayla really _____ in the office when she announced she was quitting.

6. Sorry I didn't call you on Friday like I promised. I meant to, but I got _____ with a lot of important e-mails.

7. When I was at the airport, I _____ an old classmate of mine who I hadn't seen in ten years.

8. These days, I'm _____ all my energy into starting a new career as a dance teacher.

9. I love to sit outside at night and watch the stars _____ in the sky.

10. Professor Mahmoud has been a _____ at the university for more than forty years.

11. I haven't decided what I'm going to do on my vacation yet, but I _____.

12. Laura Lane had a _____ career in the movies, and acted with all the greatest stars of the 1950s.

13. I often _____ clothes with my sister, because it's fun to wear something different for a change.

B Write replies using expressions with *hat*.

1. A: Is Ana shy about singing in front of people?

   B: No, not at all. She'll do it _____.

2. A: I'm getting a new job next month, but don't tell anyone.

   B: Don't worry. I'll _____.

3. A: I got 100% on the English exam!

   B: I have to _____ to you. It was really hard!

4. A: Jason is the owner of the restaurant, and also the chef.

   B: If he _____ like that, it must keep him really busy.

5. A: Did you hear that Jennifer Lopez has a new boyfriend?

   B: That rumor is totally _____. Tell me something I don't know!

2 GRAMMAR

A You had a long phone conversation with your aunt yesterday. Report the things she said, using the verbs in parentheses.

1. "What are you doing these days?" (ask)
   <u>She asked me what I was doing these days.</u>

2. "I've been spending a lot of time watching movies on TV." (say)
   _____.

3. "Your cousin Margaret is getting married next month." (tell)
   _____.

4. "When are you going to get married?" (ask)
   _____.

5. "My dog is getting fat." (mention)
   _____.

6. "You really shouldn't work so hard." (advise)
   _____.

7. "Please come over and have dinner with us on Sunday." (ask)
   _____.

8. "David and Lucy will be coming for dinner, too." (say)
   _____.

9. "Do you like baked ham?" (ask)
   _____.

10. "Remember to send your uncle a birthday card." (remind)
    _____.

B Match the reported sentence and the reason there is no tense change.

1. Joanne said she works at night _____   a. something just said
2. They said I should have gone to the movie. _____   b. habitual actions
3. My grandmother always said that silence is golden. _____   c. accepted fact
4. He said a minute ago that he isn't hungry. _____   d. should have/could have/past perfect

C Report each sentence. If no tense change is needed, tell the reason by writing *a*, *b*, *c*, or *d* from Activity B.

1. Alan: "I'm going to the coffee shop after class."
   _____.

2. Emily: "I run marathons every summer."
   _____.

3. Linda: "In 2002, I hadn't graduated yet."
   _____.

4. Harun: "People in India speak many languages."
   _____.

Ordinary People, Extraordinary Lives

| **Lesson B** | The kindness of strangers |

1 READING

A Read this story of a remarkable man.

Remarkable Lives: Lafcadio Hearn

The story sounds familiar. A young man, failing in his career, decides to make a fresh start overseas. He travels to Japan and gets a job teaching English at a college. There, he falls in love and gets married. He settles down with his Japanese wife, raises a family, and launches a successful new career writing about Japan.

What's surprising is that it all happened over one hundred years ago. The young man was an Irish writer named Lafcadio Hearn, who arrived in the Japanese city of Matsue in 1890. Over the next fourteen years, he wrote a dozen books about Japan and never left his adopted country. He even became a Japanese citizen, taking the name Yakumo Koizumi.

Born in 1850 and raised in Dublin, Hearn had led a difficult life before his journey to Japan. He was the son of an Irish military officer and a Greek woman, who went back to her country, **abandoning** her husband and child. When the army sent his father to India, Lafcadio went to live with an elderly aunt. At the age of sixteen, an accident left him blind in one eye. Soon after that, his aunt lost all her money in a bad investment and was forced to send Lafcadio to live with distant relatives in Cincinnati.

Hearn held a series of **menial** jobs, finally landing a position as a newspaper crime reporter at the *Cincinnati Enquirer*. Always a difficult character, Hearn frequently clashed with his editors and was forced to move on to newspapers in Memphis, New Orleans, and New York.

Then, in 1889, *Harper's Magazine* hired him to write a series of articles on Japan. Hearn arrived in Yokohama with two suitcases. In his essay "My First Day in the Orient," he wrote about the unfamiliar sights and sounds that greeted him, from the boom of a massive temple bell down to the tiny multicolored wrapper on a package of toothpicks.

Only days after arriving in Japan, Hearn got into a **dispute** with his publishers and lost his job. With the help of other foreigners, he managed to get a government appointment to teach English at a college in Matsue, a small city on Japan's west coast. He used the last of his money to get there.

He fell in love with Matsue and soon married a local woman. After years of wandering, he felt he had come home. He wrote with affection of the details of life in Matsui, like the stone fox statues in the Shinto shrine that he passed every morning on his way to school and the lovely sunsets over Lake Shinji in the center of the city.

As the only foreigner in remote Matsue, Hearn **immersed** himself in the Japanese way of life. He wore Japanese clothing, ate Japanese food, and lived in an old-fashioned Japanese house. With help from his wife, he collected and translated hundreds of traditional ghost stories. He traveled to tiny villages and ancient temples, recording everything he saw.

Many of the author's belongings are now preserved in his former home in Matsue. Alongside his books and pens are more personal treasures—his collection of Japanese tobacco pipes, a bamboo cage for his pet crickets, a seashell that his wife bought for him on an excursion. Visitors can see a stack of old newspapers with English lessons for his children written on them with a Japanese brush: "He is, she is, we are, you are good."

Hearn was writing at a **pivotal** time in Japanese history. The country was opening its doors to the modern world, and ways of life thousands of years old were changing fast. Electricity was replacing candlelight, and the first railroad line was crossing the country. In his books, he struggled to record traditional Japan before it disappeared.

Though Hearn's work has largely been forgotten, we owe a great deal to the remarkable man who first introduced the rich culture of traditional Japan to the world.

B Circle *T* for *true* or *F* for *false*. Write the phrase or sentence from the reading that supports your answer.

1. Hearn was a very successful writer in the United States.   T F

   _____.

2. Hearn often had trouble getting along with people.   T F

   _____.

3. Hearn had serious problems with his vision.   T F

   _____.

4. Hearn adjusted easily to life in his new country.   T F

   _____.

5. Hearn's books are very popular today.   T F

   _____.

6. Hearn planned to return to America one day.   T F

   _____.

7. Japanese society was modernizing rapidly when Hearn was writing.   T F

   _____.

8. Hearn's children spoke two languages.   T F

   _____.

9. Hearn wrote with interest about the modernization of Japan.   T F

   _____.

C Find the meaning of the boldfaced words in the article from their context.

1. **Abandoning** probably means _____.

   a. bringing along   b. leaving behind   c. inviting

2. A **menial** job is probably _____.

   a. badly paid   b. interesting   c. well paid

3. **Dispute** probably means _____.

   a. contract   b. argument   c. discussion

4. **Immersed** probably means _____.

   a. avoided   b. got into   c. spent money

5. **Pivotal** probably means _____.

   a. important   b. peaceful   c. forgotten

A Number the sentences to put this biography of champion bicycle racer Lance Armstrong in the correct order. Two sentences do not belong in the biography because they are not relevant. Mark them with an *X*.

_____ a. The next year, he led the first American team ever to win the Tour de France, the world's biggest cycle race.

_____ b. Lance Armstrong is the most famous and successful bicycle racer the world has even known.

_____ c. His heart is so strong that it beats only thirty-two times per minute when he's resting.

_____ d. He was born in Texas on September 18, 1971.

_____ e. In succeeding years, his team went on to win the Tour de France seven successive times, a new world record.

_____ f. Just as his career was taking off, he was diagnosed in 1996 with a deadly form of cancer that had spread throughout his body.

_____ g. At the age of thirteen, he won the Iron Kids Triathlon, and he became a professional athlete at sixteen.

_____ h. In 1998, he returned to racing and won a number of important European races.

_____ i. He announced his retirement from racing in 2005, after his seventh victory.

_____ j. He decided to specialize in cycling, and began training with the U.S. Olympic team while he was still in high school.

_____ k. He speaks fluent French and can carry on a conversation in several European languages.

_____ l. After graduation, he began spending eight months every year competing in Europe.

_____ m. Only five months after treatment, he began training again.

_____ n. He now devotes his time to his family and to raising money for cancer research organizations.

B Read this information about Nobel Peace Prize winner Wangari Maathai and write a biography. Choose the most relevant and interesting facts. You do NOT need to use all of the information.

Full name: Wangari Muta Maathai

Founder: Green Belt Movement (1976)

Member of Kenyan Parliament: 2002–present

Number of trees planted: 30 million

Born: April 1, 1940

New organization: Jubilee 2000 Africa Campaign

Bachelor's degree: biological sciences, Mount St. Scholastica College, Kansas, United States

Doctorate: University of Nairobi, 1971

Winner: 2004 Nobel Peace Prize

Occupation: Professor of Veterinary Anatomy, University of Nairobi

Marital status: divorced

First woman in East Africa to earn a Ph.D.

Family: Three children (Waweru, Wanjira, and Muta)

Active in National Council of Women of Kenya, 1976–87

Purpose of Green Belt Movement: to plant trees and preserve the environment

Countries with local Green Belt Movement: Tanzania, Uganda, Malawi, Lesotho, Ethiopia, Zimbabwe

Purpose of Jubilee 2000: to cancel the debts owed by the poorest countries

Birthplace: Nyeri, Kenya

Nickname: Mama Miti ("mother of trees")

Elected to Kenyan Parliament: 2002 (98% of votes)

Supports: democracy, human rights, and environmental conservation

Language Summaries

Unit 1 Big Screen, Small Screen

Lesson A

Vocabulary Focus

blockbuster	nerve-wracking
B-movie	shot on location
distracting	strike a
drawback	compromise
give away	tearjerker
guilty pleasure	wholesome
mainstream	

Additional Vocabulary

be a sucker for	indie
(something)	life-threatening
car chases	illness
chick flick	special effects
daring stunts	superhuman
failed romance	forces

Language Focus

Such and *so*

Speaking:

Managing a discussion

Sorry, I'm not sure I understand.
Why do you say that?
Can you clarify your reason?

Can I just add something here?
I have a point I'd like to make.
Sorry to interrupt, but . . .

To get back to our topic . . .
Let's hear what someone else has to say.
We only have five minutes left.

Lesson B

Vocabulary

addictive
authentic
average Joe
compelling
contestant
contrived
cutthroat
disturbing
dramatic
entertaining
heartfelt
inspiring
nerdy
scripted
shocking
staged
unrehearsed

Unit 2 The World Awaits You

Lesson A

Vocabulary Focus

atmosphere	hypnotic
bustling	landscape
guarantee	relatively
firsthand	relish
household names	take in

Additional Vocabulary

ageless	meaningless
childless	powerless
countless	priceless
effortless	timeless
have (something)	up for
to oneself	(something)

Language Focus

Past modals

Speaking:

Using polite language

How may I direct your call?
I'd like to speak with someone
  in Reservations, please.
Certainly.
One moment, please.
This is Cassandra.
How may I help you?
Could you please tell me the cost of a
  double room?
I'm afraid that's a little out of my
  price range.
I was wondering whether your hotel is
  located on the beach or not.
Would you mind spelling that for me?

Lesson B

Vocabulary

buy an idea
commune with nature
can-do
rooted
show-off
sorted out
surreal
wanderlust

Unit 3 *School and Beyond*

Lesson A

Vocabulary Focus

apprehensive	hectic
bond with	mishap
compulsory	rash
cope with	sign up
drop out	sleep deprivation
expectation	stick to

Additional Vocabulary

accept	except
ace (something)	it seems like a blur
advice	loose
advise	lose
affect	passed
effect	past

Language Focus

Hope and *wish*

Speaking:
Interviewing phrases

That's an interesting question.
Let me think about that a moment.
Just so that I understand, what you're
 asking is . . .

What I meant was . . .
What I'm trying to say is . . .
Let me put it another way.

What do you mean by . . . ?
When you asked . . . , did you mean . . . ?
Are you asking about . . . ?

Lesson B

Vocabulary

apply
a solid foundation
coeducational (coed)
coherent
cram school
cultivate
foster
goofing off
I couldn't agree more
so be it

Unit 4 *Contemporary Issues*

Lesson A

Vocabulary Focus

churn out	monopoly
compensate	panic
consumer	pending
crack down	rip off
emerge	take to court
greedy	unauthorized
mediocre	unethical

Additional Vocabulary

be all for (something)
(it) opened my eyes
remains to be seen
see eye to eye
see the light
see what I can do
turn a blind eye
wait and see

Language Focus

Past and present unreal conditions

Speaking:
Expressing an opinion

I strongly believe . . .
I'm convinced that . . .
Without a doubt, . . .

For instance . . .
Take, for example, . . .
To give you an idea . . .

Not only that, but . . .
Not to mention the fact that . . .
And besides, . . .

Lesson B

Vocabulary

beat (someone) up
behind my back
clash
combat
confront
dork
dreading
fitting in
get into a brawl
harass
insecure
intimidate
keep an eye on (someone)
lose your temper
lost it
opponent
pick on
threaten

Language Summaries

Unit 5 *In Other Words*

Lesson A

Vocabulary Focus

brush up on	passable
carry on	primary
convey	language
halting	proficient
immerse	retain
master	rusty
mother tongue	

Additional Vocabulary

AC (air-conditioning)
ASAP (as soon as possible)
ASL (American Sign Language)
ATM (automated teller machine)
PIN (personal identification number)
TBA (to be announced)
TGIF (thank G-d it's Friday)
whim

Language Focus

Reduced adverb clauses

Speaking:
Talking about charts and data

This chart explains . . .
As you can see, . . .
The key point is that . . .
It's clear that . . .
It's important to note that . . .
This ___ represents . . .
This ___ stands for . . .
This ___ shows . . .
This ___ describes . . .
This ___ compares . . .

Lesson B

Vocabulary

build rapport
converse
dismissive
dominate
perceive
upshot

Unit 6 *Ordinary People, Extraordinary Lives*

Lesson A

Vocabulary Focus

apprentice	juggle
aspiration	renowned
blessing	sidetracked
bump into	storied
cause (quite)	swap
a (stir)	have something
channel	in mind
fall into	twinkle
fixture	

Additional Vocabulary

at the drop of a hat
hooked on (something)
keep it under (one's) hat
old hat
take my hat off to (someone)
wear two hats

Language Focus

Reported speech

Speaking:
Presentation phrases

Today, I'm going to talk to you about . . .
I'd like to tell you about . . .
In this presentation, I'm going to . . .

Before I finish, let me say . . .
So in conclusion . . .
To conclude, . . .

Lesson B

Vocabulary

cram into	ragged
crumple	rancid
dart	rapid-fire
desperate	sandwich between
disoriented	scarce
filthy	sibling
get out in time	stain
hang out	stampede
impassable	stranded
logistics	stuff (something)
make it	under
malnutrition	submerge
meager	sweep away

Grammar Summaries

Unit 1 *Big Screen, Small Screen*

Language Focus: *such* and *so*

Use *such* and *so* to express emphasis:
> It's *such* a beautiful day!   He's *so* happy in his new job.

Use *such* before a noun:
> She has *such* energy for a 90-year-old!

Use *so* before an adjective or an adverb. If the adjective is followed by a noun, use *such* instead:
> It was *so* scary.   You walk *so* fast that I can't keep up!
> It was *such* a scary movie that I couldn't watch it.

So can be followed by a determiner *(much, little, many, few)* and a noun:
> *So* many Hollywood movies have predictable endings.

So can have the same meaning as *very*. However, since *very* cannot be followed by a *that* clause, use *so* in those cases:
> I was *so* disappointed when I failed the exam. (= *very disappointed*)
> He was *so* sleepy that he fell asleep during the movie.

Unit 2 *The World Awaits You*

Language Focus: Past modals

Use past modals (also called "perfect modals") for actions or situations that were not realized in the past or have not been realized:
> I **should've saved** more money. Now I'm broke. (expresses regret)
> We **would've taken** a taxi, but we couldn't find one. (shows willingness to do something)
> They **could've left** a message on your cell phone. (shows possibility)
> The post office **couldn't have been** open yesterday because it was a holiday. (shows impossibility)
> He **must've left** already. His coat is gone. (shows a logical conclusion)

Could have and *should have* can also be used to make suggestions and give strong advice:
> You **could've phoned** earlier. You knew my number. (mild judgment)
> You **should've phoned** earlier. I've been worried sick about you! (stronger judgment)

Couldn't have can show the speaker's disbelief at an unexpected situation:
> You **couldn't have paid** $1,000 for that plane ticket! That's too much money.

Unit 3 *School and Beyond*

Language Focus: *Hope* and *wish*

Use *hope* + simple present to describe a present or future desire or expectation. (The verb after *hope* usually takes *not* in negative sentences.) Use *hope* + *will* for future expectations only:
> I *hope* I **pass** my driver's test.   I *hope* I **don't fail** my driver's test.
> I *hope* she**'ll graduate** on time.

Use *hope so* and *hope not* in short answers:
> Is she coming to the party?   I *hope so*. I'd love to see her. / I *hope not*. I don't like her.

Use *wish + would* to express annoyance or dissatisfaction:

Please sit down. (to make a suggestion)   I *wish* you**'d** sit down. (to show annoyance)

Use *wish* + simple past / past continuous to express desire for a change in a present situation:

I *wish* you **didn't yell** at the children so much. (wanting the person to change his/her behavior)

Use *wish* + past perfect to express regret about a past situation. Use *wish + could / would* + base form to express desire for a different situation in the future:

I *wish* I **hadn't taken** that cruise.   I *wish* I **could get** a refund and use the money for something else.

Unit 4 *Contemporary Issues*

Language Focus: Past and present unreal conditionals

Use the present unreal conditional for present or future situations that are improbable. In the *if* clause, the verb can take the simple past, past continuous, or *could* + base form. Use *would/could/might* + verb in the result clause:

If they **allowed** me to download music for free, **I'd do** it. (But they *don't* allow downloading, so I won't do it.)
I **would be** too tired to enjoy school if I **took** five classes this semester.
If I **could take** a trip anywhere in the world, **I'd visit** the North Pole.
If she **were passing** all her classes easily, **I'd suggest** that she skip a grade. (But she's not doing so well in some of her classes, so I won't suggest skipping a grade.)

Use the past unreal conditional for situations in the past that could have happened but didn't. In the *if* clause, the verb is in the past perfect. Use *would have* + verb in the result clause. If you're uncertain about the result, use *might have* or *could have*:

If downloading music for free **had been allowed**, they **wouldn't have been arrested**. (But it *wasn't* allowed and so they *were* arrested.)
If I **had been traveling** in the U.K. then, **I might have been caught** in the airport workers' strike.
I **would've called** the police if **I'd seen** anything suspicious.

Unit 5 *In Other Words*

Language Focus: Reduced adverb clauses

Adverb clauses of time and reason tell when or why something happened. Those beginning with the subordinators *after, before, since, while* and *because* can be reduced to phrases that modify the main clause in a sentence:

After finishing his work, he drove home.
(adverb clause)   (main clause)

Reduced time clauses can appear in different places in a sentence. Note the use of punctuation. The reduced pattern is typically "subordinator + V-*ing*" except with the passive:

He's lost 5 kilos since he started the diet. = He's lost 5 kilos **since starting the diet.**
While I was waiting for the bus, I read. = **While waiting for the bus**, I read.
After he was found guilty, he was sentenced. = **After being found guilty**, he was sentenced.

Reduced clauses of reason do not include the subordinator. Clauses of reason with *because* and *since* can only be reduced if they are in the initial position:

Since she had studied German, she offered to translate. = **Having studied German**, she offered to translate.

Because we didn't have a map, we got lost. = **Not having a map**, we got lost. (We got lost not having a map.)

If the subjects of the main and adverb clauses are different, you cannot reduce the adverb clause:

The phone rang while we were talking.   (The phone rang while talking.)

Language Focus: Reported speech

Reported speech (also called *indirect speech*) is used to report what someone else has said. A clause that includes a reporting verb (e.g., *say* or *tell*) introduces a reported statement. The verb in the reported statement usually shifts to a past form. Quotation marks are not used with reported speech:

Quoted speech	**Reported speech**
"The meeting **is** on Friday," he said.	He said (that) the meeting **was** on Friday.

The reporting verb *say* can be followed immediately by a reported statement. Reporting verbs that behave like *say* are *announce, explain, mention,* and *report*. The reporting verb *tell* is always followed by an indirect object and then the reported statement. Reporting verbs that behave like *tell* are *advise, instruct, persuade,* and *remind*. The words in parentheses can be omitted:

"I never went to college," she said.   She *explained* (to us) (that) she **had** never **been** to college.
                                         She *reminded* us (that) she **had** never **been** to college.

With reported commands, use an appropriate reporting verb + the infinitive:

"Stretch for five minutes before exercising."   He *said* **to stretch** five minutes before exercising.
                                                He *advised* us **to stretch** five minutes before exercising.

Pronouns and time adverbs also shift in reported speech:

"I'll call you when I **arrive** in Paris later today," said Sabina. She said (that) she would call me when she **arrived** in Paris yesterday.

Ask and *want to know* are used to report questions. Use *if* or *whether* with *yes/no* questions. Statement-word order is used in the reported question. Question marks are not used:

Yes/No question	"Are you running in the marathon this weekend?"	He *asked* (me) *if* / *whether* I was running in the marathon (or not). He *wanted* to know *if* / *whether* I was running in the marathon (or not).
Wh-question	"Where do you go to school, Daniel?"	She *asked* (him) *where* he went to school. She *wanted* to know *where* he went to school.

Skills Index

Grammar
- *-ed* endings, 5
- Expressing opinions, 44
- *happens to,* 43
- *hope* and *wish,* 28–29
- *-ing* endings, 5
- Interviewing phrases, 30
- Low possibility, 43
- *make, allow,* and *let,* 29
- Past and present unreal conditionals, 42–43
- Past modals, 16–18
- Presentation phrases, 68
- Reduced adverb clauses, 54–55
- Reported speech, 66–67
- *say* and *tell,* 66
- *should (happen to) . . . might,* 43
- *such* and *so,* 4–5
- Text organization using contrasts, 58
- *were to,* 43
- *wh-* questions, 67
- *wish,* showing regret in the past, 18
- *see* and *watch,* 13

Listening
- Conversations, 27
- Descriptions, 16
- Films, 3
- Interviews, 3, 41, 65–66
- Sales pitches, 11
- TV shows, 53
- Skills
  - Asking and answering questions, 3, 8, 15, 16, 20–21, 27, 31, 33, 39, 41, 46, 53, 58, 66, 67, 69, 70

Reading
- Announcements, 30
- Articles, 9, 22, 40, 43, 46–47, 58–59, 64, 70–71
- Biographies, 72
- Blurbs, 14
- Brochures, 35
- Charts, 11, 28, 42, 54, 65
- Conversations, 16, 18
- Descriptions, 11, 73
- E-mail messages, 57
- Essays, 34
- Excerpts, 4
- Interviews, 20–21, 26, 44, 67
- Letters, 18, 42, 67
- Online postings, 2, 32–33
- Opinions, 52
- Predictions, 41
- Presentations, 68
- Profiles, 52
- Quotes, 19
- Reports, 60
- Reviews, 4,10
- Sentences, 17, 54, 75
- Statements, 58
- Stories, 17, 23
- Summaries, 8
- Tips, 30
- TV guide, 7
- Skills
  - Guessing meaning from context, 70
  - Inferring author's opinion or attitude, 8
  - Matching questions with answers, 21

Prereading activities, 7, 19, 31, 45, 57, 69
- Scanning, 32, 58
- Understanding text, 46
- Using contrasts, 58

Speaking
- Asking and answering questions, 3, 8, 15, 16, 20–21, 23, 27, 31, 33, 39, 40, 41, 46, 53, 58, 66, 67, 69, 70
- Conflict resolution, 49
- Debating, 61
- Describing, 5, 23, 45, 67, 69
- Discussing, 7, 11, 14, 18, 19, 23, 30, 31, 35, 41, 44, 45, 48, 49, 52, 56, 57, 65, 68, 69, 70, 72, 73
- Explaining, 7, 11, 17, 35, 42, 77
- Expressing opinions, 44
- Interviewing, 11, 30
- Making a reservation, 18
- Managing discussions, 6
- Polite language, 18
- Presentations, 68
- Reporting to class, 6, 23, 44
- Retelling stories, 64, 70
- Role playing, 5, 18, 26, 29, 30, 39, 44, 49, 61, 77
- Sales pitches, 11

Topics
- Conflict resolution, 45–49
- Feature films, 2–6
- Follow your dream!, 64–68
- In the city, 40–44
- The kindness of strangers, 69–73
- New school, old school, 31–35
- On the road, 14–18
- School life, 26–30
- Talk to me, 57–61
- There and back, 19–23
- Total immersion, 52–56
- TV time, 7–11

Viewing
- Charts, 56, 77
- CNN® videos, 11, 23, 35, 49, 61, 73
- Illustrations, 31
- Photographs, 16, 20–21, 45, 64, 69, 77

Vocabulary
- *abroad,* 24
- *accent,* 63
- *ace (something),* 26
- Acronyms, 53
- *Actions speak louder than words,* 74
- *argument,* 51
- *ASL (American Sign Language),* 52
- *audience,* 13
- *average Joe,* 9
- *be all for (something),* 40
- *be a sucker for,* 2
- *blockbuster,* 2
- *B-movie,* 2
- *buy an idea,* 21
- Charts and data, 56
- *chick flick,* 2
- *class,* 37
- *coeducational (coed),* 34
- *commune with nature,* 23
- *conflict,* 51

contestant, 9
- Contrasts, 58
- *couldn't agree more,* 32
- *course,* 37
- *cram school,* 32
- *critic,* 13
- *critique,* 13
- *dialect,* 63
- *dork,* 47
- *drive,* 25
- *educate,* 36
- *eminent,* 75
- *excellent,* 75
- *exceptional,* 75
- *extraordinary,* 75
- *faculty,* 37
- *famous,* 75
- *fight,* 51
- *get out on time,* 71
- *glamour,* 62
- *grammar,* 62
- Guessing meaning from context, 69
- *have seen the light,* 41
- *have (something) to oneself,* 14
- *hooked on (something),* 64
- *humor,* 12
- *illegal,* 51
- *indie,* 2
- Initialisms, 53
- *instructor,* 37
- *it seems like a blur,* 26
- *jargon,* 63
- *A journey of a thousand miles begins with a single step,* 24
- *keep an eye on (someone),* 47
- *lack,* 51
- *language,* 63
- *-less* ending, 15
- *lesson,* 37
- *lost it,* 47
- *mainstream,* 2
- *major,* 37
- *make it,* 71
- *motorist,* 25
- *nerdy,* 9
- *notorious,* 75
- *odd,* 75
- *opened my eyes,* 41
- *passenger,* 25
- *professor,* 37
- *remains to be seen,* 41
- *renowned,* 75
- *review,* 13
- *sail,* 25
- *saw eye to eye,* 41
- *see what I can do,* 41
- *see/watch,* 13
- *show off,* 21
- *sibling,* 71
- *slang,* 63
- *so be it,* 33
- *spectators,* 13
- *squeaky wheel gets the grease, The,* 50
- *strange,* 75
- Suggesting compromise, 49
- *teacher,* 37
- *tearjerker,* 2
- *terminology,* 63

tourist, 25
travel, 25
traveler, 25
turned a blind eye, 41
tutor, 37
unauthorized, 51
unethical, 51
uninterested, 51
unusual, 75
up for (something), 15
viewers, 13
wait and see, 41
whim, 52

Writing
   Answers to questions, 17, 20–21, 48
   Articles, 22
   Biographies, 72
   Brochures, 35
   Charts, 4, 8, 27, 28, 31, 36, 39, 46,
      70, 77
   Interviews, 30
   Lists, 30, 34
   Online posts, 48
   Opinion essays, 34
   Questions, 20–21, 30
   Reports, 60
   Reviews, 10
   Scenes for plays, 55
   Sentences, 4, 28, 43, 67
   Topic sentences, 10
Skills
   Editing, 22, 34, 60
   Expressing opinions, 48
   Note taking, 3, 27, 35
   Sentence completion, 4, 15, 24, 25,
      29, 32, 37, 41, 46, 50, 51, 53, 58, 62,
      63, 68, 70, 74, 75, 76
   Thesis statements, 34

Student Book Answer Key

Page 6, 4 Speaking, Activity B: Pair Work
Answers: 1. Oscar, **2.** France, **3.** British Academy of Film and Television Arts,
4. 1982

Page 7, 1 Getting Ready to Read, Activity A: Pair Work
Answer: 1. *Blind Love* is not actually a reality TV show.

Page 19, 1 Getting Ready to Read, Activity B: Pair Work
Answers: 1. largest, **2.** English, **3.** Soccer, **4.** oil, **5.** hot and spicy, **6.** the
musician Sade

Page 23, 4 Communication, Activity B: Pair Work
Answer: The Baileys were rescued by the crew on the Weolmi,
a Korean fishing boat.

Page 57, 1 Getting Ready to Read, Activity A: Pair Work
Answer: The first e-mail, at left, was written by a woman. The second
e-mail, at right, was written by a man.

Expansion Pages Answer Key

Unit 1   Pages 12–13
A. 1. credits **2.** dubbed **3.** soundtrack **4.** subtitled **5.** on location
6. flashback **7.** stunts **8.** studios **9.** screenplays **B. 1.** g **2.** h **3.** c
4. f **5.** b **6.** a **7.** e **8.** d **C. 1.** with **2.** second **3.** small
4. large **5.** about **6.** number **7.** between **8.** and (plus) **D. 1.**
genuine **2.** spin-off **3.** episode **4.** distracted **5.** vie **6.** producer
7. footage **8.** nasty **E. 1.** remote **2.** networks **3.** cable
4. channels **5.** satellite **6.** antenna **7.** show **8.** host

Unit 2   Pages 24–25
A. 1. missed **2.** delayed **3.** caught **4.** called **5.** canceled
6. got in **7.** diverted. **B. 1.** f **2.** g **3.** a **4.** j **5.** c **6.** i **7.** e **8.** b
9. d **10.** h **C. 1.** stamped **2.** show your **3.** apply for **4.** a valid
5. an expired **6.** renew **7.** check **D. 1.** a bat **2.** an ox **3.** a feather
4. a beet **5.** night **6.** a mouse **7.** a bone **8.** snow **9.** a bee
10. nails

Unit 3   Pages 36-37
A. 1. i **2.** b **3.** h **4.** j **5.** d **6.** f **7.** g **8.** e **9.** c **10.** a
B. Positive: I aced it, I passed, I did well   Negative: Don't ask, I failed,
I flunked, I did very poorly, I bombed   Informal: Don't ask, I aced it. I
flunked, I bombed **C. 1.** seminary **2.** law school **3.** medical school
4. art academy **5.** university **6.** technical college **7.** dental school
8. military academy **D. 1.** c **2.** h **3.** f **4.** b **5.** a **6.** g **7.** d **8.** e
E. 1. higher education **2.** primary education **3.** physical education
4. Secondary education **5.** pay for his education **6.** adult education
7. standard of education **8.** get an education

Unit 4   Pages 50-51
A. 1. peace talks **2.** a symbol of peace **3.** live in peace **4.** a peace
treaty **5.** a threat to peace **6.** the peace process **7.** work(s) for peace
8. a plea for peace **B. 1.** revitalize **2.** slum **3.** unchecked
4. proposition **5.** engage in **6.** Overall **7.** widespread **8.** forefront
9. advocate **10.** sustainable **C. 1.** c **2.** a **3.** g **4.** d **5.** i **6.** b
7. e **8.** h **9.** f **D. 1.** I've heard that one before. **2.** turned a deaf
ear **3.** are up to our ears **4.** heard it through the grapevine **5.** lends
a sympathetic ear **6.** I'm all ears. **7.** grinning from ear to ear **8.** it
went in one ear and out the other **9.** has the ear

Unit 5   Pages 62-63
A. 1. pointless discussion **2.** broaden the discussion **3.** a heated
discussion **4.** generate a discussion **5.** under discussion
6. take part in a discussion **7.** a great deal of discussion **B. 1.** sign
language **2.** difficult **3.** lose **4.** verb **5.** passable **6.** speech
C. 1. g **2.** c **3.** f **4.** d **5.** b **6.** a **7.** h **8.** e **D. 1.** interrupts
2. dominates **3.** feedback **4.** widespread **5.** upshot **6.** dismissive
7. perceive **8.** build rapport **E. 1.** already **2.** illegal **3.** OK
4. develop **5.** occurred **6.** OK **7.** professor **8.** safety **9.** receive
10. affect **11.** definite **12.** twelfth **13.** succeed **14.** government
15. disappear **16.** jewelry **17.** assistant **18.** unbelievable **19.** OK
20. necessary

Unit 6   Pages 74-75
A. 1. d **2.** b **3.** f **4.** g **5.** h **6.** a **7.** e **8.** c **B. 1.** How's life? **2.** a
new life **3.** save your life **4.** risk their lives **5.** a matter of life and
death **6.** Life's too short. **7.** lost their lives **8.** my social life **C. 1.** e
2. g **3.** c **4.** a **5.** f **6.** b **7.** d **D. 1.** stranded **2.** impassable
3. immaculately **4.** disoriented **5.** scarce **6.** submerged **7.** filthy
8. upheaval **E. 1.** generous **2.** unfriendly **3.** strange **4.** intelligent
5. dishonest **6.** annoying

Impressão e Acabamento   Jan / 2006   Prol EDITORA GRÁFICA